Bibliotheca Persica

Persian Heritage Series
Number 36

Nāṣer-e Khosraw's
Book of Travels

Center for Iranian Studies
Columbia University, New York

Persian Heritage Series

The Persian Heritage Series aims at making Persian literary, historical and scientific texts available in translation. The translations in the series are intended not only to satisfy the needs of the students of Persian history and culture, but also to respond to the demands of the intelligent reader who seeks to broaden his intellectual and artistic horizons through an acquaintance with major world literatures.

General Editor
Ehsan Yarshater (Columbia University)

Advisory Council
I. Gershevitch (Cambridge University)
G. Lazard (University of Paris)
B. Spuler (University of Hamburg)
R. N. Frye (Harvard University)

Late Members
A. J. Arberry (Cambridge University)
W. B. Henning (University of California)
H. Massé (University of Paris)
T. C. Young (Princeton University)
G. Morgenstierne (University of Oslo)
G. Tucci (University of Rome)

The volumes in the Persian Heritage Series form part of the
UNESCO COLLECTION OF REPRESENTATIVE WORKS.

A current list of the published titles in the Persian Heritage and related series appears at the end of this volume.

Persian Heritage Series

Edited by Ehsan Yarshater

Number 36

Nāṣer-e Khosraw's

Book of Travels

(Safarnāma)

Translated from Persian,
with introduction and annotation by

W. M. Thackston, Jr.

Senior Preceptor in Persian
Harvard University

Bibliotheca Persica

Published by

The Persian Heritage Foundation under
the imprint of Bibliotheca Persica

Printed in the United States of America

For information, address State University of New York Press, State University Plaza, Albany, N.Y., 12246

Library of Congress Cataloging in Publication Data

Nāṣer-e Khosraw, 1004-ca. 1088.
The book of travels = (Safarnáma)

(Persian heritage series; no. 36)
Translation of: Safarnamah.
Includes index.
1. Near East—Description and travel. I. Thackston, W. M. (Wheeler McIntosh), 1944– . II. Title.
III. Title: Safarnāma. IV. Series.
DS46.N313 1985 915.6′044 85–4657
ISBN 0–88706–067–6
ISBN 0–88706–066–8 (pbk.)

10 9 8 7 6 5 4 3 2 1

Contents

Preface

Nāṣer-e Khosraw, the well-known Persian poet, moralist and theologian was a mundane, prosperous and wine-loving bureaucrat in the Saljuq administration, until 1045, when a visionary dream brought to a head his latent tendencies and transformed him overnight into a devoted man of faith. The following year he planned a pilgrimage to Mecca which was eventually extended into a seven year journey. It took him from Marv in northeastern Persia to Nishābur, Rayy, and Azerbaijan and then through Armenia and eastern Anatolia to Syria and Palestine and finally to Mecca. He returned, however, to Jerusalem and took the route by land and sea to Egypt, where he became fascinated by the country's prosperity and its orderly administration under the Fatimids. It was here apparently that he embraced the Isma'ili doctrine.

After visiting Mecca three more times and returning to Egypt twice, he finally headed for his home country by going to south Yemen, crossing the arabian desert to Basra in southern Iraq, and then by way of Isfahan to Balkh in modern Afghanistan. The *Safarnāma* or Book of Travels is a record of this journey.

Nāṣer soon, however, found himself harrassed by the Sunni authorities and took refuge in the nearby village of Yomgān, where he lived in forced retirement at least for 15 years, devoting his time to writing and to intense Isma'ili missionary activity.

A man of considerable culture and curiosity, Nāṣer-e Khosraw met in the course of his travels with many people, wondered at many monuments and public buildings, and set down his observations in his travel book. Written in a concise style sometime resembling an abridgement, and enlivened from time to time by Nāṣer's dry sense of humor, the *Safarnāma* contains many keen and valuable observations on peoples and places, as well as on the economic and social conditions of countries that he visited. In his lively descriptions, Cairo, Jerusalem, and Mecca and their monuments stand out. His account of a small "communistic" Carmathian city-state in al-Ahsā's near Bahrain is of special interest.

Despite its reputation, the *Safarnāma*, had never been translated into English in its entirety, Guy LeStrange's translation of the sections on Syria and Palestine (Pilgrim's Text Society, volume IV, London: 1883) having remained a partial rendering. The present complete translation by Dr. Wheeler Thackston is accompanied by a glossary of proper names, places, and terms, all in vigorous transliteration for the benefit of specialists, and an appendix listing the places visited by Nāṣer, together with a map of the route followed by him, as well as explanatory notes, which are designed to help those interested in philological, historical, and geographical aspects of the text.

Ehsan Yarshater

Introduction

While on an official trip in the autumn of 1045, Nāser, son of Khosraw of Qobādiyān (Marv District in northeastern Khorasan), by his own account, experienced a dream-vision that jolted him out of a "forty-year sleep of heedlessness" and awakened in him a desire to abandon the life of a civil administrator for a "quest for truth." Several months after this experience Nāser obtained a leave of absence from his post and, ostensibly intending to make a pilgrimage to Mecca, settled his debts and set out from Marv toward Nishāpur, the cultural capital of Khorasan. However, instead of joining a caravan bound for the Hejaz, he began a peregrination that took him across the Caspian coast of Iran, into eastern Anatolia and down into Syria and Palestine. Although he did make a pilgrimage from Jerusalem, he did not return to his native Khorasan but rather retraced his steps to Jerusalem and thence made his way to Egypt and Cairo, the seat of the Fatimid caliphate. From Egypt he made his way to the Hejaz, across the Arabian peninsula and through Iran to return, some seven years after his departure, to his home in Balkh. The record of his adventures, observations and experiences is contained in his travelogue, the *Safarnāma*.

Of Nāser's life we have little information, and of his early years practically nothing is known. From the fact that both he and his brother Abu'l-Fath ʿAbd al-Jalil were employed in governmental service (the brother is mentioned in the *Safarnāma* as a member of the entourage of Abu Nasr, vizier to the prince of Khorasan), it may be inferred that the family belonged to the clerical/administrative class that regularly supplied the bureaux of state with those of its young men who had attained through rudimentary schooling a competence in the "three R's." That Nāser was not rigorously trained in the religious and theological "Arabic" sciences of a systematic Islamic education is evident in his philosophical works.[1]

It is known of Nāser that at some point in his life he embraced

[1]See V. A. Ivanow, *Nasir-i Khusraw and Ismailism* (Leiden: Brill, 1948). For an evaluation of Naser-e Khosraw's contribution to Ismaili thought, see Henry Corbin, "Nasir-i Khusraw and Iranian Isma'ilism," in *The Cambridge History of Iran,* vol. 4, Ed. R. N. Frye, pp. 520–542.

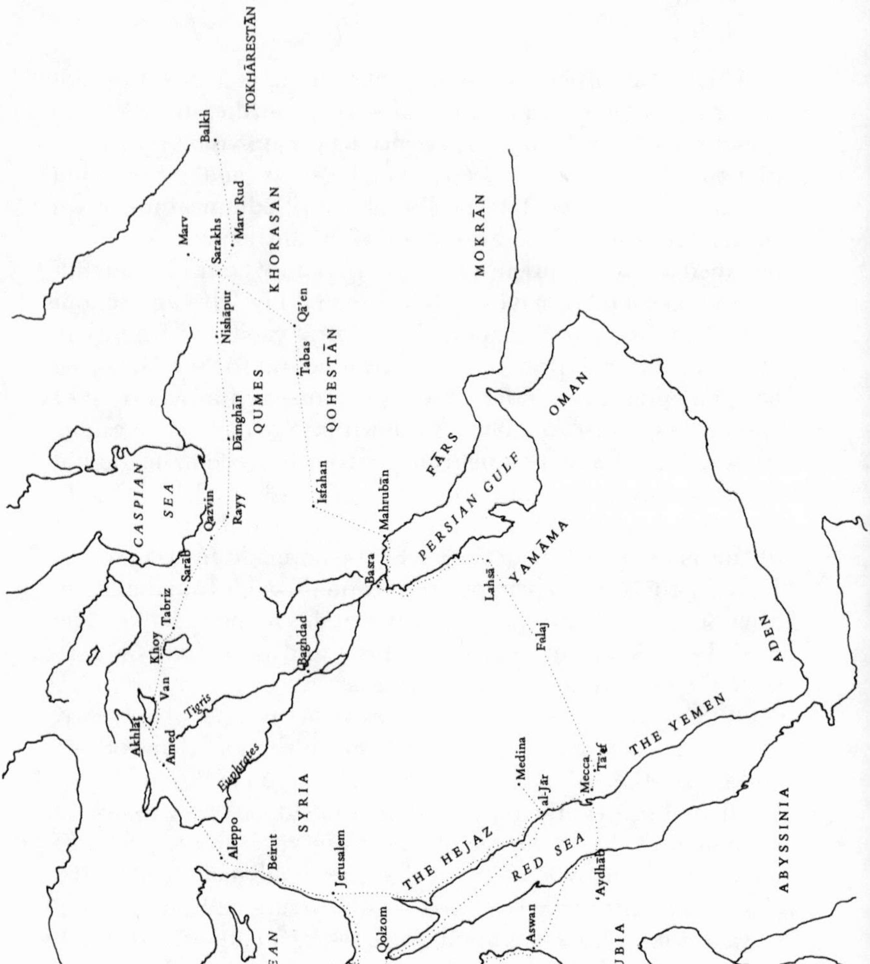

TOKHĀRESTĀN
Balkh
Marv
Sarakhs
Marv Rud
KHORASAN
MOKRĀN
Nishāpur
Qā'en
Tabas
QOHESTĀN
QUMES
Dāmghān
CASPIAN
SEA
Qazvin
Rayy
Isfahan
Mahrubān
FĀRS
OMAN
PERSIAN GULF
Sarāb
Tabriz
Khoy
Van
Akhlat
Amed
Tigris
Euphrates
Basra
Baghdad
Lahsā
YAMĀMA
Falaj
ADEN
THE YEMEN
Medina
Mecca
Ta'ef
al-Jār
SYRIA
Aleppo
Beirut
Jerusalem
THE HEJAZ
RED SEA
'Aydhāb
ABYSSINIA
Aswan
NUBIA
Qolzom
Cairo
Nile
EGYPT
MEDITERRANEAN
SEA

Ismailism, which cause he served actively as missionary in the Caspian region of Iran and later as exile in Yomgān (Badakhshān), writing treatises and poetry, where he is last known to have been in 1061. Although it cannot be proved, it makes good sense to assume that his conversion to Ismailism took place before he set out on the journeys described in the *Safarnāma,* for he made in effect a tour of every important center of Ismailism west of Transoxania, and the only places upon which he expends favorable comment throughout his travels are those ruled by Ismailis. If he was not being sent from one Ismaili stronghold to another, there is little to justify his eccentric skirting of the central Islamic world. And he makes no attempt to explain himself. He was not a rich man who could indulge himself in *Wanderlust*: he mentions once or twice in passing that he was accompanied only by a brother and one Indian servant. His observations of all he saw constantly betray the civil administrator: he admires fortifications, waterworks, strategic situations of towns, prices, etc. He was obviously captivated by monumental architecture and pomp and circumstance: the Dome of the Rock shrine complex at Jerusalem and the mosque precincts at Mecca are meticulously described, as are the public displays of Fatimid ceremony in Cairo. He mentions rare and delightful fruits and vegetables he encounters, he converses with unusual persons in out-of-the-way places, and he never misses an opportunity to visit a saint or prophet's shrine. Yet there is little in his narrative that would characterize him as a professional traveler or a particularly interested observer of the people he met or the places he visited.

The Ismaili sect, to which Nāser belonged from at least middle age and for which he worked and wrote in his later years, was at this period in its history actively engaged in propaganda and conversion. The movement had originated as a schism from Shiʿism, the branch of Islam that recognized as the only legitimate successors to the Prophet Muhammad and interpreters of the revealed law the lineal descendants of the Prophet through his daughter Fātema and her husband ʿAli b. Abi Tāleb. Because of a difference of opinion over the seventh imam, the Ismailis split from the majority of the Shiʿa, whose line of imams continued down to the twelfth and who are consequently known as "Twelvers," whereas the Ismaili line continued on. In Nāser's time the twelver branch of Shiʿism had recently entered into its eschatological phase with the Greater Occulation of the representatives of the Twelfth Imam in 940, and the Twelver Shiʿites had no capital or power base of their own from which to direct propaganda. There were, however, numerous Shiʿite pockets scattered throughout the Islamic world, notably in Daylam and Tabarestān (through which Nāser passed) and in Transoxania, of which Nāser makes no mention whatsoever.

The Sevener, or Ismaili, branch of Shiʿism, by contrast, had ruled Egypt since the Fatimid conquest in 969 and ran its covert and overt propaganda machine from Cairo, where Nāser spent a goodly portion of his seven-year absence from his homeland. There he was most likely being trained in missionary techniques.

In Transoxania and eastern Iran, at precisely the time that Nāser left his administrative post and began his travels, the power of the Seljuk Turks was rapidly spreading: Marv had capitulated to them in 1037, and Herāt and Nishāpur in 1038, and Balkh and Tokhārestān were taken in 1040. Unlike their predecessors the Ghaznavids, the Seljuks, who were adamant Sunnis, were actively opposed to all forms of Shiʿism and were determined to rid their territory of all Shiʿite opposition. If he was already an Ismaili, it is not at all unlikely that the advent of the Seljuks into Khorasan had something to do with Nāser's decision to absent himself from the province.

In his travelogue Nāser does not touch upon theological or sectarian debates, and he makes scant mention of the political turmoils of the time. Yet his observations on the places he visited give us an interesting, if superficial, view into the eleventh-century Islamic world. More importantly they provide us with an insight into a personality of that time. Generally speaking, aside from the facts and figures Nāser records, most of which are easily found elsewhere, what he chooses to convey to his reader tells us more about himself than it does about what he saw and gives us a rare glimpse into the attitudes of a man from an age very different from our own.

The Travelogue of Nāser-e Khosraw

Thus writes Abu Moʿin Hamid al-din Nāser son of Khosraw of Qobādiyān in the district of Marv:

I was a clerk by profession and one of those in charge of the sultan's revenue service. In my administrative position I had applied myself for a period of time and acquired no small reputation among my peers.

In the month of Rabiʿ II in the year 437 [October 1045],[1] when the prince of Khorasan was Abu Solaymān Chaghri Beg Dāud son of Mikā'il son of Saljuq, I set out from Marv on official business to the district of Panj Deh in Marv Rud, where I stopped off on the very day there happened to be a conjunction of Jupiter and the lunar node. As it is said that on that day God will grant any request made of him, I therefore withdrew into a corner and prayed two *rakʿats*, asking God to grant me true wealth. When I rejoined my friends and companions, one of them was reciting a poem in Persian. A particular line of poetry came into my head, and I wrote it down on a piece of paper for him to recite. I had not yet handed him the paper when he began to recite that very line! I took this to be a good omen and said to myself that God had granted my behest.

From there I went to Juzjānān, where I stayed nearly a month and was constantly drunk on wine. (The Prophet says, "Tell the truth, even if on your own selves.") One night in a dream I saw someone saying to me, "How long will you continue to drink of this wine, which destroys man's intellect? If you were to stay sober, it would be better for you."

In reply I said, "The wise have not been able to come up with anything other than this to lessen the sorrow of this world."

"To be without one's senses is no repose," he answered me. "He cannot be called wise who leads men to senselessness. Rather, one should seek out that which increases reason and wisdom."

"Where can I find such a thing?" I asked.

"Seek and ye shall find," he said, and then he pointed toward the *qebla* and said nothing more. When I awoke, I remembered

[1]See Appendix A on Islamic dates.

everything, which had truly made a great impression on me. "You have waked from last night's sleep," I said to myself. "When are you going to wake from that of forty years?" And I reflected that until I changed all my ways I would never find happiness.

On Thursday the 6th of Jomādā II of the year 437 [19 December 1045], which was by Persian reckoning the middle of the month of Day, the last month before the year 414 of the Yazdgerdi era,[2] I cleansed myself from head to foot, went to the mosque, and prayed to God for help both in accomplishing what I had to do and in abstaining from what he had forbidden.

Afterwards I went to Shoburghān and spent the night in a village in Fāryāb. From there I went via Samangān and Tālaqān to Marv Rud and thence to Marv. Taking leave from my job, I announced that I was setting out for the Pilgrimage to Mecca. I settled what debts I owed and renounced everything worldly, except for a few necessities.

On the 23rd of Shaʿbān [5 March 1046] I set out for Nishapur, traveling from Marv to Sarakhs, which is a distance of thirty parasangs. From there to Nishapur is forty parasangs.

On Saturday the 11th of Shawwāl [21 April] I came to Nishapur. On Wednesday, the last day of the month, there was a lunar eclipse. The prince at this time was Toghrel Bēg Mohammad, brother to Chaghri Bēg. He had ordered a school built near the Saddlers' Bazaar, which was being constructed then. He himself had gone to Isfahan for his first conquest of that city.

On the 2nd of Dhu'l-Qaʿda I left Nishapur and, in the company of Khwāja Mowaffaq, the sultan's agent, came to Qumes via Gavān. There I paid a visit to the tomb of Shaikh Bāyazid of Bestām.

On Friday the 8th of Dhu'l-Qaʿda [17 May] I went out to Dāmghān. The first of Dhu'l-Hejja 437 [9 June 1046] I came to Semnān by way of Ābkhwari and Chāshtkhwārān, and there I stayed for a period of time, seeking out the learned. I was told of a man called Master ʿAli Nasā'i, whom I went to see. He was a young man who spoke Persian with a Daylamite accent and wore his hair uncovered. He had a group of people about him reading Euclid, while another group read medicine and yet another

[2]The Persian Yazdgerdi era was calculated from the beginning of the reign of Yazdgerd III, the last Sasanian shah of Iran (A.D. 632). See Appendix A.

mathematics. During our conversation he kept saying, "I read this with Avicenna," and "I heard this from Avicenna." His object of this was, of course, for me to know that he had been a student of Avicenna. When I became engaged in discourse with some of these people, he said, "I know nothing of arithmetic [*siyāq*] and would like to learn something of the arithmetic art." I came away wondering how, if he himself knew nothing, he could teach others.

From Balkh to Rayy I reckoned the distance to be 350 parasangs. From Rayy to Sāva is said to be thirty parasangs, from Sāva to Hamadān thirty, from Rayy to Isfahan fifty, and to Āmol thirty. Between Rayy and Āmol is Mount Damāvand, which is shaped like a dome and is called Lavāsān. They say that on the top of the mountain is a pit from which ammonia is extracted, and also sulphur. Leather skins are hauled up and filled with ammonia, and when full they are rolled down the mountainside, there being no road over which they can be transported.

On the 5th of Moharram 438 [12 July 1046], corresponding to the 10th of Mordād 415 of the Persian calendar, I set out for Qazvin and came to the village of Quha, where there was a drought. A maund of barley bread was being sold for two dirhems. [Displeased,] I left.

On the 9th of Moharram [16 July] I arrived in Qazvin, which has many orchards with neither walls nor hedges, so that there is nothing to prevent access to the gardens. I thought Qazvin a nice city: its walls were well fortified and furnished with crenellations, and the bazaars were well kept, only water was scarce and limited to subterranean channels.[3] The head of the city was an Alid. Of all the trades practiced in the city, shoemaking had the largest number of craftsmen.

On the 12th of Moharram 438 [19 July 1046] I left Qazvin along the road to Bil and Qapān, village dependencies of Qazvin. From there my brother, a Hindu slave-boy we had with us, and I came to a village called Kharzavil. As we had few provi-

[3]The "subterranean channels" of which Nāṣer speaks were formerly called *kārēz* (today called *qanāt*) and are still in use for bringing water for irrigation from distant sources. Many of these channels have been maintained from ancient times, such as the one mentioned on page 101; see Mohammad al-Karagi, *La Civilisation des eaux cachées*, ed. and trans. with commentary by Aly Mazaheri, Université de Nice, Institut d'Etudes et de Recherches Interethniques et Interculturelles, Etudes Preliminaires 6 (Nice: I.D.E.R.I.C., 1973).

sions, my brother went into the village to buy some things from the grocer. Someone asked him, "What do you want? I'm the grocer."

"Whatever you have will be all right with us," said my brother, "for we are strangers passing through." Yet whatever edibles he mentioned, the man only said, "We don't have any." From then on, wherever we saw anyone like this man, we would say, "He's the grocer from Kharzavil!"

Passing on from there, we encountered a steep descent. Three parasangs farther was a village belonging to Tāram called Baraz-al-Khayr [?]. It was tropical and had many pomegranate and fig trees, most of which grew untended. Passing on, we came to a river called Shāhrud, on the banks of which was a village called Khandān, where a toll was levied for the duke, who was one of the Daylamite kings. As this river passes through this village, it joins with another river called Sapidrud. When these two rivers have united, the water flows down into a valley to the east of the mountains of Gilān, then on to Gilān itself and finally empties into the Caspian Sea. They say that fourteen hundred rivers spill into the Caspian, the circumference of which is said to be twelve hundred parasangs. In the midst of the sea there are islands with many inhabitants, as I heard from many people.

But let me return to my own story. From Khandān to Shamirān there are three parasangs of desert that is quite rocky. The latter is the metropolis of Tāram. Beside the city is a high fortress, the foundation of which is laid on solid granite. It is surrounded by three walls, and in the middle of the fortress is a water channel connected to the river, the water of which is drawn up into the fortress. There are a thousand sons of the aristocracy kept inside that fortress so that no one can rise up in rebellion. It is said that the prince has many such fortresses in Daylam and that he rules with such complete justice and order that no one is able to take anything from anyone else. When the men go to the mosque on Fridays, they all leave their shoes outside, and no one steals them. The prince signs himself thus on paper: "Ward of the march of Daylam, the *gil* of Gilān, Abu Sāleh, client to the Prince of the Faithful." His name is Jostān Ebrāhim.

In Shamirān I saw a good man from Darband whose name was Abu Fadl Khalifa, son of ʿAli the Philosopher, He was a wor-

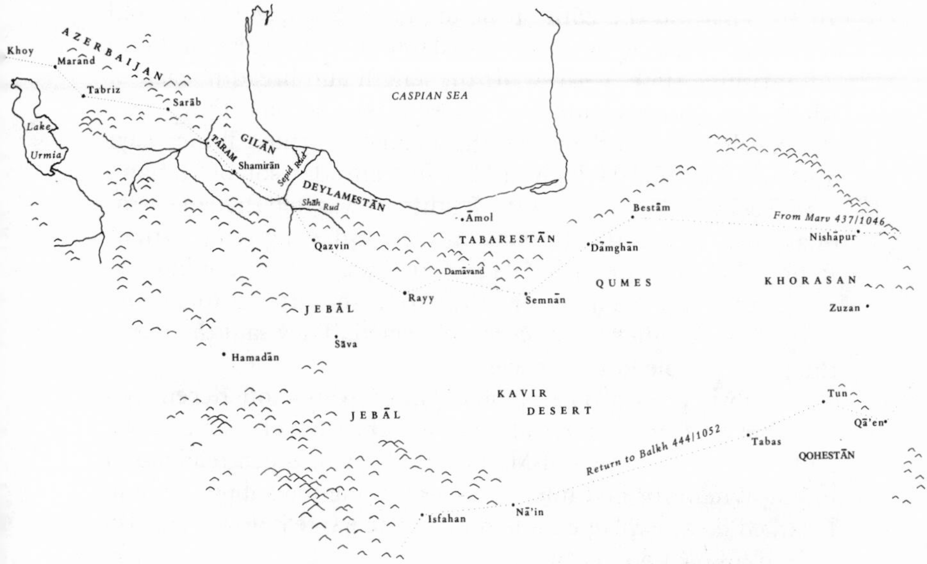

Naser's route of travel through northern Iran

thy fellow and displayed much generosity and nobility of character to us. We discoursed together, and a friendship sprang up between us.

"Where do you intend to go from here?" he asked me.

"My intention is to make the Pilgrimage," I said.

"What I desire," he replied, "is that on your return journey you pass through here so I may see you again."

Azerbaijan and Beyond

On the 26th of Moharram [2 August] I left Shamirān. On the 14th of Safar [20 August] I arrived in Sarāb. On the 16th of Safar [22 August] I parted from Sarāb and, passing through Saʿidābād, arrived in Tabriz on the 20th of Safar 438 [26 August

1046]. That was the 25th of the month of Shahrivar by the old reckoning. This city is the principal town of Azerbaijan and is in a flourishing state. I paced off the length and breadth, each of which was fourteen hundred paces. In the sermon they name the padshah of Azerbaijan in this manner: Exalted Prince Sayf al-Dawla Sharaf al-Mella Abu Mansur Vahsudān son of Mohammad, client to the Prince of the Faithful. I was told that an earthquake had occurred in this city on Wednesday night the 17th of Rabiʿ I 434 [4 November 1042], which was during the intercalary days. After the night prayer, part of the city was totally destroyed while other parts were unharmed. They said that forty thousand people lost their lives.

In Tabriz I saw a poet named Qatrān, who wrote decent poetry, but he could not speak Persian very well. He came to me and brought the works of Manjik and Daqiqi, which read aloud to me. Whenever he came across a meaning too subtle for him, he asked me. I explained it to him and he wrote it down. He also recited his own poetry to me.

On the 14th of Rabīʿ I [18 September] I parted from Tabriz on the Marand road and, accompanied by one of Prince Vahsudān's soldiers, came to Khoy. From there also I traveled with a courier up to Bargri. From Khoy to Bargri is thirty parasangs. We arrived on the 12th of Jomādā I [14 November]. From there we came to Vān and Vastān, where they sell pork in the bazaar as well as lamb. Men and women sit drinking wine in the shops without the slightest inhibition. From there we arrived in the city of Akhlāt on the 18th of Jomādā I [20 November]. This city is the border town between the Muslims and the Armenians, and from Bargri it is nineteen parasangs. The prince, Nasr al-Dawla, was over a hundred years old and had many sons, to each of whom he had given a district. In the city of Akhlāt they speak three languages, Arabic, Persian, and Armenian. It is my supposition that this is why they named the town Akhlāt.[4] Their commercial transactions are carried on in cash money, and their rotl is equivalent to three hundred dirhems.

On the 20th of Jomādā [22 November] I left there and came to an outpost. It was snowing and extremely cold. On the plain

[4]Nāṣer thinks the name of the town is derived from the Arabic root *khalaṭa* "to mix"; it is called Khlatʿ in Armenian and was formerly known as Khelāṭ in Arabic. The derivation Nāṣer supposes is unlikely

up to the town there is a section of the road with planks laid on the ground so that on snowy and blizzardy days people can find their way over the wood. From there I went on to Betlis, which lies in a valley. We bought some honey, a hundred maunds for one dinar, at the rate they sold to us. We were told that in this town there were men who produced three to four hundred jars of honey a year.

Leaving that place, I saw a fortress called Qef Onzor, which means "stop and look." Passing on, I came to a place where there was a mosque said to have been built by Oways Qarani.

There I saw men who roamed about the mountainsides and cut a wood something like cypress. I asked what they did with it, and they explained that when one end of this wood is placed in fire, pitch comes out the other end. It is then collected in pits, put into containers, and sent all over for sale.

The regions that I have briefly mentioned after Akhlāt are dependencies of Mayyāfāreqin. We went to the town of Arzan, which is a flourishing place with running water and orchards, gardens, and good bazaars. During the Persian month of Ādhar they were selling two hundred maunds of grapes, which they call *raz-e armānush*, for one dinar.

The Region of Diyār Bakr

From there we went to Mayyāfāreqin, which is 28 parasangs distant. From Balkh to Mayyāfāreqin by the way we came was 552 parasangs. It was Friday the 26th of Jomādā I 438 [28 November 1046]. At the time the leaves on the trees were still green. The place has an enormous fortification made of white stone, each slab of which weighs five hundred maunds, and every fifty ells is a huge tower of this same white stone. The top of the rampart is all crenellated and looks as though the master builder had just finished working on it. The city has one gate on the west side set in a large gateway with a masonry arch and an iron door with no wood in it. It has a Friday mosque that would take too long to describe. Briefly, the ablution pool faces forty chambers, through each of which run two large canals, one of which is visible and is for use, while the other is concealed beneath the earth and is for carrying away refuse and flushing the cisterns. Outside of the city are caravanserais and bazaars, baths, and another congregational mosque used on Fridays. To the north is another town called Mohdatha, and it too has bazaars, a congregational mosque, and baths, all of which are well laid out. In the sermon they style the sultan of the district thus: the Great Prince ʿEzz al-Eslām Saʿd al-Din Nasr al-Dawla Sharaf al-Mella Abu Nasr Ahmad, and he is said to be a hundred years old. The rotl there is equal to 480 stone dirhems. That same prince has built a city at a distance of four parasangs from Mayyāfāreqin and called it Nasriyya. From Āmed to Mayyāfāreqin is nine parasangs.

On the 6th of Day, old reckoning, we arrived in Āmed, the foundation of which is laid on a monolith rock. The length of the city is two thousand paces, and the breadth the same. There is a wall all around made of black rock, each slab weighing between a hundred and a thousand maunds. The facing of these stones is so expert that they fit together exactly, needing no mud or plaster in between. The height of the wall is twenty cubits, and the width ten. Every hundred ells there is a tower, the half circumference of which is eighty ells. The crenellations are also of this same black stone. Inside the city are many stone stairs by means of which one can go up onto the ramparts, and atop every tower is an embrasure. The city has four gates, all of iron with no wood, and each gate faces one of the four cardinal directions. The east gate is called the Tigris Gate, the west gate the Byzantine Gate, the north the Armenian Gate, and the south the Tell Gate. Outside this wall just described is yet another wall, made of that same stone, the height of which is ten ells and the top of which is completely covered with crenellations. Inside the crenellation is a passageway wide enough for a totally armed man to pass and to stop and fight with ease. The outside wall also has iron gates, placed directly opposite the gates in the inside wall so that when one passes from a gate in the first wall one must traverse a space of fifteen ells before reaching the gate in the second wall. Inside the city is a spring that flows from a granite rock about the size of five millstones. The water is extremely pleasant, but no one knows where the source is. The city has many orchards and trees thanks to that water. The ruling prince of the city is a son of that Nasr al-Dawla who has been mentioned.

I have seen many a city and fortress around the world in the lands of the Arabs, Persians, Hindus, and Turks, but never have I seen the likes of Āmed on the face of the earth or have I heard anyone else say that he had seen its equal. The congregational mosque too is of black stone, and a more perfect, stronger construction cannot be imagined. Inside the mosque stand two-hundred-odd stone columns, all of which are monolithic. Above the columns are stone arches, and above the arches is another colonnade shorter than the first. Above that is yet another row of arches. All the roofs are peaked, and all the masonry is carved and painted with designs. In the courtyard of the mosque is placed a large stone atop which is a large, round pool of stone. It is as high as a man, and the circumference is ten ells. From the middle of the pool protrudes a brass waterspout from which shoots clean water; it is constructed so that the entrance and the drain for the water are not visible. The enormous ablution pool is the most beautiful thing imaginable—only the stone from which Āmed is built is all black, while that of Mayyāfāreqin is white. Near the mosque is a large church, elaborately made of the same stone, and the floor is laid in marble designs. Beneath the dome, which is the Christians' place of worship, I saw a latticed iron door, the likes of which I had never seen before.

From Āmed to Harrān there are two roads: along one of them are no settlements, and this one is forty parasangs long; along the other road are many villages, most of the inhabitants of which are Christian, and that way is sixty parasangs long. We went by caravan along the settled route. The plain is extremely level except for a few places so rocky that the animals could hardly go a pace without stepping on a rock.

On Friday the 25th of Jomādā II 438 [27 December 1046], or the 22nd of Day, old reckoning, we arrived in Harrān. The weather at that time was like the weather in Khorasan at Nawruz. From there we went to a town named Qarul,[5] where a young man invited us into his home. When we had come into the house, a bedouin Arab sixty years old came in and sat down next to me.

"Teach me the Koran," he said. I recited him the chapter be-

[5]"Qarul" is probably the modern Urfa, medieval Edessa. Qarul is not mentioned by the Arab geographers, however.

ginning "*Qol a'udho be-rabbe'l-nās.*" He recited it back to me. When I had said the part that goes "*mena'l-jennate wa'l-nās,*" he said, "Should I say '*a-ra'ayta'l-nās*' too?" "There is no more to this chapter," I replied. Then he asked, "Which chapter has the part in it about the *naqqālat al-hatab?*" He did not even know that in the chapter called Tabbat the words *hammālat al-hatab* occur, not *naqqālat al-hatab*![6] That night, no matter how many times I recited the chapter beginning "*Qol a'ūdho be-rabbe'l-nās,*" he could not learn it. A sixty-year-old Arab!

Into Syria

Saturday the 3rd of Rajab 438 [3 January 1047] we came to Saruj. The next day we crossed the Euphrates and arrived in Manbej, the first town you come to in Syria. It was the first of the month of Bahman in the old reckoning, and the weather was extremely pleasant. There were no buildings outside of the town. From there I went to the city of Aleppo.

From Mayyāfāreqin to Aleppo is one hundred parasangs. I found Aleppo to be a nice city. It has a huge rampart, twenty-five cubits high, I estimated, and an enormous fortress, as large as the one at Balkh, set on rock. The whole place is populous, and the buildings are built one atop another. This city is a place where tolls are levied on the merchants and traders who come and go among the lands of Syria, Anatolia, Diyār Bakr, Egypt, and Iraq.

The city has four gates: the Gates of the Jews, the Gate of God, the Garden Gate, and the Antioch Gate. The standard weight used in the bazaar there is the Zāheri rotl, which is 480 dirhems. Twenty parasangs to the south is Hamā, and after that Homs. Damascus is fifty parasangs from Aleppo; from Aleppo to Antioch is twelve parasangs, and the same to Tripoli. They say it is two hundred parasangs to Constantinople.

[6]In the first instance, the Koranic verse Nāser is trying to teach the man ends with the words *men al-jennate wa'l-nās* ("from the djinn and people"). The Arab asks, "*A-ra'ayta'l-nās?*" ("Did you see the people?"), a non sequitur that indicates he has understood nothing but the last word. In the second instance the Arab asks Nāṣer for the chapter that speaks of the "wood-carrier," but he uses a word for "carrier" other than the one used in the Koranic text.

On the 11th of Rajab [11 January] we left the city of Aleppo. Three parasangs distant was a village called Jond Qennasrin. The next day, after traveling six parasangs, we arrived in the town of Sarmin, which has no fortification walls.

Six parasangs farther on was Maʿarrat al-Noʿmān, which is quite populous. It has a stone wall. Beside the city gate I saw a cylindrical column of stone, which had something written on it in a script that was not Arabic. I asked someone what it was, and he said that it was a talisman against scorpions. If ever a scorpion were brought in from outside and turned loose, it would run away and not stay in the town. I estimated that column to be about ten ells high. I found the bazaars to be flourishing, and the Friday mosque built on a rise in the middle of town so that from whatever place one wants to go up to the mosque, one has to ascend thirteen steps. Their whole agriculture consists of wheat, which is plentiful. Figs, olives, pistachios, almonds, and grapes also abound. The city water comes from both rain and wells.

In the city was a man named Abu'l-ʿAlā' of Maʿarra. Although blind, he was the head of the city and very wealthy, with many slaves and servants. Everyone in the city, in fact, was like a slave to him, but he himself had chosen the ascetic life. He wore coarse garments and stayed at home. Half a maund of barley bread he would divide into nine pieces and content himself with only one piece throughout the entire day and night. Besides that, he ate nothing. I heard it said that the door to his house was always open and that his agents and deputies did all the work of the city, except for the overall supervision, which he saw to himself. He denied his wealth to no one, although he himself was constantly fasting and vigilant at night, taking no part in the affairs of the world. This man has attained such a rank in poetry and literature that all the learned of Syria, the Maghreb, and Iraq confess that in this age there is no one of comparable stature. He has composed a book called *al-Fosul wa'l-ghāyāt,* in which he speaks in enigmatic parables. Although eloquent and amazing, the book can be understood only by a very few and by those who have read it with him. He has even been accused of trying to rival the Koran. There are always more than two hundred persons from all over gathered about him reading literature and poetry. I have heard that he himself has composed more than a hundred thousand lines of poetry. Someone once asked him why, since God had given him all this wealth and property, he gave it away to the people and hardly ate anything himself. His answer was, "I own nothing more than what I eat." When I passed through that place he was still alive.

On the 15th of Rajab 438 [15 January 1047] we went to Kafr Tāb and thence to Hamā, a fine, populous city on the banks of the Orontes. The reason this river is called ʿĀsi ["rebellious" in Arabic] is because it runs into Byzantium, that is, when it goes from the lands of Islam to the lands of the infidels it becomes "rebellious." On the river are many water wheels. From there the road forks, one way leading along the coast through western Syria and the other to the south and Damascus. We took the coastal route.

In the mountains we saw a spring that they say flows every year after the middle of Shaʿbān.[7] For three days it flows, after which there is not a drop of water until the next year. Many people go there on pilgrimage and seek propitiation of God. They have built edifices and pools there. Passing on from that place, we came to a field covered with narcissus in bloom, and the entire place looked white because of all the flowers. Afterwards, we arrived in a town called ʿErqa. Two parassangs past ʿErqa we came to the seashore. Five parasangs to the south along the shore we came to Tripoli. From Aleppo to Tripoli is forty parasangs the way we came.

Description of Tripoli

On Tuesday the 5th of Shaʿbān [4 February] we arrived. The outskirts of the city are all agricultural, with orchards and gardens, with lots of sugar cane and many groves of oranges, citron, bananas, lemons, and dates. Just at that time they were making molasses. The city of Tripoli is so situated that three sides face the water, and when the water is rough, some of the waves lap against the city walls. On the eastern side of the city, which faces

[7]Since Islamic months are lunar (see Appendix A), the spring would begin approximately eleven days earlier each year, a fact that may have occasioned Nāṣer's comment.

dry land, they have made a large moat with a strong iron gate. The walls are of hewn stone and have battlements and embrasures, and there are balistae on top of the walls, as they live in constant dread of naval attack by the Byzantines. The area of the city is one thousand cubits square. The buildings are four and five stories tall, and there are even some of six. The lanes and bazaars are so nice and clean you would think each was a king's palace. Every type of food, fruit, and other edible I ever saw in Persia was to be found here, but a hundred times more plentiful. In the midst of the city is a well-kept, beautifully adorned, and solidly constructed mosque. In the yard is a large dome, beneath which is a marble pool with a brass fountain. In one of the bazaar streets, water spills out from five spouts for people to draw water. The excess runs down over the ground and down into the sea. There are said to be twenty thousand people in this city, and it has many villages and dependencies. They make very good paper there, like the paper of Samarqand, only better.

This city belongs to the sultan of Egypt because, as it is said, once an infidel Byzantine army came and attacked the city. The sultan of Egypt defeated that army and lifted the land tax. There are now always soldiers garrisoned there and a commander over the soldiers to protect the city from its enemies. It is also a customs station, as ships from Byzantium, Europe, Andalusia, and the Maghreb dock there. They pay ten percent to the sultan, which income provides for the soldiers' maintenance. The sultan keeps ships there that go to Byzantium, Sicily, and the Maghreb to trade. The people of this city are all Shi'ites, and the Shi'ites have built nice mosques in every land. They have edifices there like caravanserais, which they call *mashhads,* but no one lives in them. Outside the city of Tripoli there is not a single structure except for a couple of *mashhads.*

We continued south along the shore. One parasang away I saw a fort called Qalamūn, which had a spring inside. From there I went to Tarāborzon, which is five parasangs from Tripoli. Thence we went to Byblos, which is a triangular city with one angle to the sea. Surrounding it is a very high, fortified wall. All around the city are date palms and other tropical trees. I saw a child holding both a red and a white rose, both in bloom, and that was on the 5th of the last Persian month, Esfandārmadh, old reckoning, of the year 415 of the Persian calendar.

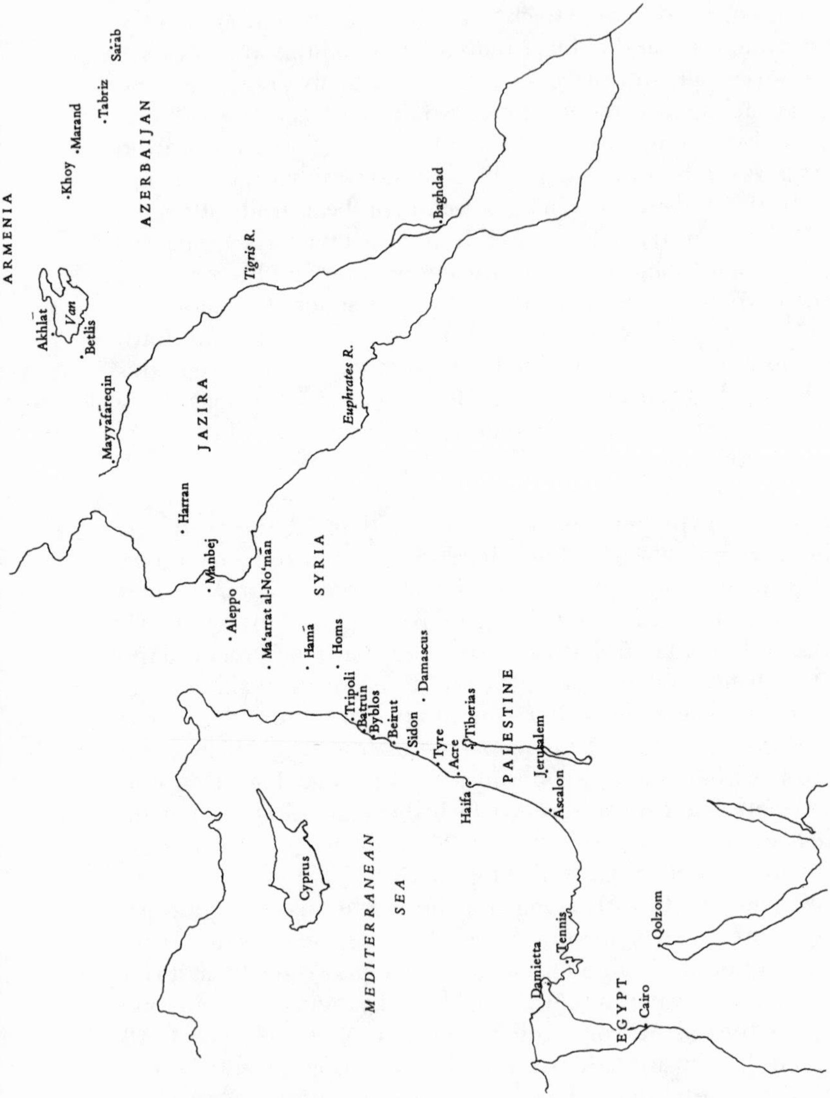

Eastern Mediterranean

Beirut, Sidon, and Tyre

From Byblos we went to Beirut, where I saw a stone arch situated so that the road ran right through it. I estimated the arch to be fifty ells high, and on all sides were slabs of white stone, each of which weighed over a thousand maunds. This edifice was made of bricks up to a height of twenty ells, and on top were set up marble cylinders, each eight ells tall and so thick that two men could scarcely reach around. On top of these columns were more arches on both sides, of such exactly fitted masonry that there was neither plaster nor mud in between. Above this was a great arch right in the middle, fifty cubits high. I estimated that each stone in that arch was eight cubits long and four wide, so that each one must have weighed approximately seven thousand maunds. All these stones had designs carved in relief—better in fact than one usually sees executed in wood. Except for this arch, no other edifice remains in that area. I asked what place this had been and was told that it is said to have been the gate to Pharaoh's garden and was extremely old. The whole plain thereabouts abounds with marble columns, capitals, and bases, all of carved marble—round, square, hexagonal, and octagonal—and of a kind of stone so hard that iron makes no impression on it. Yet there is no mountainous terrain nearby from which the stone might have been quarried, and all other stone there is soft enough to be hewn with iron. In the outlying regions of Syria there are more than five hundred thousand of these fallen columns, capitals, and bases, and no one knows what they were or from where they were brought.

From there we went to Sidon, which is also on the edge of the sea. Much sugarcane is planted there, and the city has a strong stone wall with three gates and a Friday mosque with a very pleasant atmosphere. It is covered completely with multicolored mats. The bazaar is so nicely arrayed that when I saw it I thought the city had been decorated either for the arrival of the sultan or because of the proclamation of some good news. When I inquired, they said that the city was customarily kept that way. The gardens and orchards were such that one would think an emperor had laid out a pleasure garden with belvederes, and most of the trees were laden with fruit.

Five parasangs away we came to the city of Tyre, which is located beside the sea. From the shore runs a spit on which the city is built. It is such that the walls are not more than a hundred yards on dry land, the rest being in the sea. The ramparts are all masonry, and the joints are plugged with pitch so that the seawater cannot seep through. I estimated the city to be a thousand cubits square, with buildings of five to six stories and many fountains. The bazaars are nice, and prosperity abounds. The city of Tyre is renowned among the cities of the Syrian coast for its wealth and riches. The inhabitants are mostly Shi'i. There was a judge there, however, who was Sunni by sect, named Ebn Abi 'Aqil; he was of a pleasant countenance and rich. By the city gate is a shrine furnished with many carpets, mats, and gold and silver lamps and lanterns. The town is situated on a high spot, and its water comes from the mountains. Up to the city gate are stone arches atop which water is brought into the city. Opposite the city in the mountains is a valley, and if one goes eighteen parasangs to the east, one comes to Damascus.

Acre

When we had gone seven parasangs we came to the city of Acre, which there they write 'Akkā. The city is situated on a rise, and some of the ground is uneven and sloping while other parts are level. Along the coast, they only build towns where there is elevated ground for fear of being inundated by seawater when the waves strike the shore. The Friday mosque is in the middle of the town and is on the highest spot. All the columns are marble. To the right of the *qebla,* outside the mosque, is the prophet Sāleh's tomb. The courtyard of the mosque is partially paved in stone and partially planted with grass. They say that Adam cultivated that very spot. I measured the city, the length of which was two thousand cubits and the breadth five hundred. The walls are extremely strong, and the southwestern portion is on the sea. To the south is a *minā.* Most of these coastal towns have a *minā*, which is like a stable for ships. Built right against the town, it has walls out into the water and an open space of fifty ells without a wall but with a chain stretched from one wall to the other.

When a ship is about to enter the *minā,* they loosen the chain so that it goes beneath the surface of the water, allowing the ship to pass over; afterwards the chain is raised again lest strangers make untoward attempts on the ships. To the left of the eastern gate is a spring, to get to which one must descend twenty-six steps. This spring is called the Cow Spring, and they say that Adam discovered it and watered his own cattle from it, whence it derives its name.

To the east of Acre is a mountain where various prophets' shrines are located, but this place is off the main road to Ramla. I had an intention to see these holy pilgrimage sites and to gain God's blessings from them, but the people of Acre told me that there were evil people along the way who would set upon a stranger and take whatever he might have. What valuables I had I deposited therefore in the Acre mosque and set out from town by the eastern gate. Early on Saturday the 23rd of Shaʿbān 438 [22 February 1047] I visited the tomb of ʿAkk, the founder of Acre, who had been a great and pious man. Since I had no guide with me to show me the way, I had become confused, when suddenly, thanks to God's great goodness, I chanced upon a Persian man from Azerbaijan who had visited those holy sites before and had returned a second time. I prayed two *rakʿats* in thanks to God and rendered thanks to Him for giving me a companion so that I could fulfill the intention I had made.

Then I came to a village called al-Berwa, where I visited the tombs of Esau and Simeon. Next I came to a small cave they called Dammun, which I visited too, since they say it is the tomb of Dhu'l-Kefl. Then I came to a village named Eʿbellin, where they claim is the tomb of Hud. I made a visit. Inside the enclosure is a mulberry tree. The tomb of the prophet Ezra, which I visited, is there also.

Heading south, I came to another village called Hazira, to the west of which is a valley where there is a freshwater spring flowing from a rock. Next to the spring was a mosque built on a rock, and inside were two stone chambers with stone roofs and a door so small that it was difficult to enter. Inside are two adjacent tombs, one of Jethro and the other of his daughter, Moses' wife. The people of this village keep up the mosque and shrine very well, cleaning them and maintaining the lamps. Next I came to a village called Irbid, to the south of which was a hill with an enclosure containing the tombs of four of Jacob's sons, brothers of Joseph. Proceeding farther, I saw a hill in which was a cave containing the tomb of Moses' mother. I made a visit and then went on through a valley, which ends at a small sea, along the shore of which is located the city of Tiberias. The sea is about six parasangs long and three wide, and the water is fresh and potable. The city is on the western side of the sea, and all the bath and sewage water empties into the sea, yet the people of the town and shore district all drink from the water of the sea.

I heard that once a prince of this city ordered the sewage drains that emptied into the sea stopped up. When they did this, the water turned so foul it wasn't fit to drink. He then ordered the drains reopened, and the water became good again. This town has a fortified wall extending from the shoreline all around the town; there is no wall on the water side. There are many buildings in the water, and the bed of the lake is rock. They have made belvederes on the top of the marble columns that are in the water. The lake is full of fish.

The town has a Friday mosque; by its gate is a spring with a bathhouse over it. The water is so hot that unless it is mixed with cold water you cannot stand it. They say that it was built by Solomon, and I went inside to try it out.

On the west side of the city of Tiberias is a mosque called the Jasmine Mosque, which is exceptionally fine. Right in the middle of the mosque is a large platform containing several niches; around the platform are jasmine bushes, which is why it is so called. On the east side is a colonnade containing the tomb of Joshua son of Nun. Beneath the platform are the tombs of the Seventy Prophets who were slain by the children of Israel. To the south of the city is the Dead Sea, the water of which is salty, although it is south of Tiberias and the fresh water of the Sea of Galilee flows into it. Lot's city was on the shore of this sea, but no trace of it remains. I heard from someone that in the bitter waters of the Dead Sea is something shaped like a cow that grows up from the bottom and resembles stone, but not so hard.[8] It is gathered, broken into pieces, and peddled around in the towns because one piece of it planted at the base of a tree will keep

[8]A type of water moss known in Persian as *gāvāb* ("water-ox"), called *toḥlob* and *thawr al-mā'* in Arabic. See Moḥammad Ḥosayn b. Khalaf Tabrizi, *Borhān-e qāṭe'*, ed. Moḥammad Mo'in (Tehran: Ebn-e Sinā, 1330-42/1951-63), vol. 3, p. 1766.

worms from attacking the roots and will repel underground vermin from a whole orchard. This, at any rate, is what I was told. Druggists also buy it because a worm called *noqra* that gets into medicines is repelled by this substance. In the town of Tiberias they make reed prayer mats sold there for five dinars.

To the west of Tiberias is a mountain where there is a piece of granite inscribed in Hebrew to the effect that at the date of inscription the Pleiades were on the edge of Aries. The tomb of Abu Horayra is there also, outside the city to the south, but no one can go there because the people are Shiʿi and whenever anyone does go, the children make a racket, attack, and harass and throw stones. For this reason I was unable to visit that place. Upon returning I came to a village called Kafr Kannā; on the top of a hill to the south there is a cell with an immovable door, said to be the tomb of the prophet Jonah. By the door to the cell is a freshwater well. Having made my visit, I returned to Acre, a distance of four parasangs. We remained in Acre for one day more and then left.

From Acre to Jerusalem

We came to a village called Haifa. Along the village road is much sand of the type used by Persian goldsmiths, which they call *makki* [Meccan]. The village of Haifa is on the coast and has many palm groves and orchards. The shipbuilders there make large seagoing vessels they call *judi.*

One parasang from there is another village called Kanisa, where the road turns away from the coast toward the hills. To the east are desert plains called the Valley of Crocodiles. After a parasang or two, the road again joins the coast. Here we saw the bones of many sea animals that had been fossilized because of constant pounding by waves. Seven parasangs from Acre, we came to a town called Caesarea, a nice place with running water, palm groves, orange and citron groves, and a fortified rampart with an iron gate. There are springs inside the town and a Friday mosque so situated that when seated inside one can look out over the sea. There is a marble vase there as thin as Chinese porcelain, although it holds a hundred maunds of water.

Saturday the last of Sha'bān [28 February 1047] I left there. For one parasang there was that Meccan sand, then once again we saw many fig and olive trees. All along the way the hills and plain were planted with trees. Having gone a few parasangs, we arrived in a town called Kafr Sābā and Kafr Sallām. From here to Ramla is three parasangs, the whole way orchards, as I have said.

Sunday the first of Ramadān [1 March] we arrived in Ramla, which is eight parasangs from Caesarea. It is a large town with a fortified rampart of stone and mortar, tall and strong, with iron gates. From the city to the shore is three parasangs. Their water supply is rainwater, and inside every building are pools to collect it so that there will be a constant supply. In the Friday mosque there are large pools from which anyone can draw water when they are full. I measured the courtyard and found it to be three hundred paces by two hundred. Across a porch was an inscription to the effect that on the 15th of Moharram 425 [10 December 1033] there was a violent earthquake that destroyed many buildings, but no people were injured.

There is much marble here, and most of the buildings and houses are made of sculpted marble. They cut the marble with toothless saws and Meccan sand. The saw is drawn along the length of the shaft, not across the grain, as with wood. From the stone they make slabs. I saw all colors of marble—speckled, green, red, black, white, and multicolored. There is a kind of grape there that is better than grapes elsewhere and is exported all over. The city of Ramla is said to belong to Syria and western Palestine.

On the 3rd of Ramadān [3 March] we left Ramla and came to a village called Laṭrun.[9] Farther on we came to a village called Qaryat al-'Enab. All along the way I noticed great quantities of rue growing wild. We saw a spring with very good fresh water flowing out of rock; it was made with troughs all around and had several outbuildings about. From there we started up a hill as though ascending a mountain, on the other side of which one would expect to come down to a city. Once we had gone up a way, however, a vast plain came into view, partially rocky and partially soil. Atop the hill is the city of Jerusalem. From Tripoli,

[9]All manuscripts give Khātun; Schefer observes that it should be Laṭrun.

which is on the coast, to Jerusalem is 56 parasangs. From Balkh to Jerusalem is 876 parasangs.

Jerusalem

The 5th of Ramadān 438 [5 March 1047] we entered Jerusalem. It had been one solar year from the time we left home, and throughout our travels we had not stopped anywhere long enough to have rested completely.

Jerusalem, which the people of Syria and that region call "Qods," is visited during the season by people of the area who are unable to make the Pilgrimage to Mecca. They perform the requisite rituals and offer a sacrifice on the customary holiday. Some years more than twenty thousand people come during the first days of Dhu l-hejja bringing their children to celebrate their circumcision. From the Byzantine realm and other places too come Christians and Jews to visit the churches and synagogues located there. The large church will be described later.

The outlying villages and dependencies of Jerusalem are all in the hills, and all cultivation, olives, figs, and so on, is totally without irrigation, yet prosperity is widespread and prices cheap. There are villagers who collect each up to five thousand maunds of olive oil in pits and tanks to be exported all over the world. They say there has never been a faminine in the land of Syria, and I heard from reliable sources that a great man once saw the Prophet in a dream and said, "O Prophet of God, assist us in our livelihood!" In response the Prophet said, "The bread and olives of Syria are with me."

A General Description of Jerusalem

Now I will describe the city of Jerusalem. It is situated on top of a hill and has no source of water save rain. The villages, on the other hand, have springs, but there are none inside the city. Around the city is a fortified rampart of stone and mortar with iron gates. Near the city there are no trees, since it is built on rock. It is a large city, there being some twenty thousand men there when I saw it. The bazaars are nice, the buildings tall, and the ground paved with stone. Wherever there was a rise or hill it has been graded down level so that when it rains the whole ground is washed clean. There are many artisans in the city, each group having its own separate quarter. The eastern wall is attached to the congregational mosque.

Passing out of the mosque you come out onto a large, expansive, and flat plain called Sāhera. They say that this is where the Resurrection will take place, where all men will be gathered together. For this reason many people have come there from all over the world and taken up residence in order to die in that city. When God's appointed time comes, they will already be in the stipulated place. O God! on that day wilt Thou be Thine own servants' protector and Thy mercy. Amen. O Lord of the universe!

On the edge of the plain is a large cemetery, where there are many spots in which men pray and make special requests, which are granted by God. O God, receive our supplications and forgive our sins and evil deeds. Have mercy upon us, O Most Merciful!

Between the cathedral mosque and the Plain of Sāhera is a large, deep valley shaped like a trench. Therein are large edifices laid out by the ancients. I saw over the door of one house a carved stone dome, and a thing more amazing than this could scarcely exist: I could not figure out how it had been raised. Everybody said it was Pharaoh's House and that this was the Valley of Gehenna.[10] I asked how it came to be called thus and was told that, in the days of the caliphate of Omar, the Plain of Sāhera had been the site of an army camp. When Omar looked at that valley, he said, "This is the Valley of Gehenna." The common people say that anyone who goes to the edge of the valley can hear the voices of the people in hell. I went there but heard nothing.

Half a parasang south of the city, one goes down a hill to a spring, called ʿAyn Selwān [the Spring of Siloam], that flows from rock. They have built many buildings around it, and it

[10]The Valley of Gehenna is known in Judeo-Christian sources as the Valley of Jehoshaphat. "Gehenna" (Arabic *jahannam*) is the Islamic proper name for Hell.

waters the gardens. They say that whoever washes in that water will be cured of chronic illness. Much has gone into pious endowment for that spring.

Jerusalem has a fine, heavily endowed hospital. People are given potions and draughts, and the physicians who are there draw their salaries from the endowment.

The Sanctuary of Jerusalem

The hospital and Friday mosque are on the eastern side of the city, and one wall of the mosque[11] is on the Valley of Gehenna. Looking at the wall from outside the mosque, one can see that it is one hundred cubits high and made of large, unmortared stones. Inside the mosque [area] the top of the wall is level. The mosque was built in that place because it is the site of the very rock which God commanded Moses to make the direction of prayer. When this commandment came, Moses did make it the direction of prayer; not long thereafter he died. Then, in the time of Solomon, as that rock was still the direction of prayer, the mosque was built around the rock, with the rock in the middle. This rock remained the direction people faced for prayer until the time of the Prophet Mohammad, when God commanded the direction to be toward the Kaʿba [in Mecca], a description of which will come in its proper place.

I wanted to measure the dimensions of this sanctuary, but I thought that first I should get a general idea of the plan and layout, after which I could make my measurements. For a long time I wandered about the area, looking at it from different vantages. Then, on the northern side, near the Dome of Jacob, I discovered an inscription in stone over an arch to the effect that the length of this sanctuary is 704 cubits and the width 455 cubits in royal ells (the royal ell being what is called the *gaz-e shāyegān* in Khorasan, and equivalent to slightly less than 1½ ells). The ground of the area is paved with stone and the joints are filled with lead.

[11]Throughtout this section Nāṣer refers to the entire precincts of the Ḥaram al-Sharif, the sanctuary of the Dome of the Rock and al-Aqṣā Mosque, as "the mosque" (*masjed*).

The sanctuary is located to the east of the city and bazaar, so that to get to it from the bazaar one goes east. It has a splendid gateway, thirty ells high and twenty wide, from which two "wings" open out on each side. The gateway, the facing of the wings, and the open hall of the gateway are adorned with designs and patterned with colored tiles set in plaster. The whole produces an effect dazzling to the eye. There is an inscription on the tiles of the gateway with the titles of the sultan of Egypt. When the sun strikes this, the rays play so that the mind of the beholder is absolutely stunned. Over the gateway is a huge dome made of stone, with two ornate doors set therein. The facing on these doors is of Damascene brass and looks like gold. They are covered with designs and are fifteen ells high and eight wide. These doors are called the Bāb Dāud [Gate of David].[12] Inside and to the right of these doors you find two great colonnades, each of which has twenty-nine marble pillars with capitals and bases of colored marble, with lead-caulked joints. Over the columns are masonry arches placed one atop the other, without mortar, such that each arch contains no more than four or five blocks of stone. These colonnades run to near the *maqsūra*. To the left of the doors, that is, to the north, is a long colonnade with sixty-four arches atop marble columns and another gate called Bāb al-Saqar [Gate of Hell]. The length of the mosque extends from north to south, to where the *maqsūra* opens out, but the shape of the court is square, with the *qebla* to the south.

On the north side are two more adjacent doors, each of which is seven ells wide and twelve high. These doors are called Bāb al-Asbāt [Gate of the Tribes]. Beyond these doors, which are along the breadth of the sanctuary leading eastward, there is another

[12]The following correlation between the gates of the sanctuary mentioned by Nāṣer and gates as they are today has been made by Sir C. W. Wilson (Appendix C in Le Strange's translation of the Palestine section of the *Safarnāma*, pp. 67–72): Nāṣer's Bāb Dāud is the Bāb al-Selsela; the gate called al-Saqar by Nāṣer is thought to be the modern Bāb al-Nāẓer; Nāṣer's Bāb al-Asbāṭ is now known as Bāb al-Ḥeṭṭa; the Bāb al-Abwāb of Nāṣer's text is the modern Bāb al-Asbāṭ; the gate leading to the Sufis' Cloisters should be the modern Bāb al-ʿAtm; the double gates of Bāb al-Raḥma and Bāb al-Tawba are the modern Golden Gate; Nāṣer's Bāb al-Nabi should be the Gate of the Old Aqṣā; the Bāb al-ʿAyn may be the modern Single Gate or Triple Gate, now closed; the Bāb al-Ḥeṭṭa, so called by Nāṣer, should be the now closed Bāb al-Nabi, also known as Bāb al-Borāq; and what Nāṣer refers to as the Bāb al-Sakina is known as the Bāb al-Salām and adjoins the Bāb al-Selsela.

huge gateway containing three adjacent doors of the same dimensions as the Gates of the Tribes. All are ornately done in iron and brass of the best workmanship imaginable. This gate is called Bāb al-Abwāb [Gate of Gates] because in all other places the gateways come in pairs, and this gate alone is triple.

Between these two gateways, on the northern side, in a colonnade in which the arches rest on solid pillars, is a dome supported by tall columns and decorated with lamps. It is called Jacob's Dome, as it is supposed to have been his place of prayer. On the broad side of the mosque is another colonnade, and in the wall is a doorway. Outside that are the cloisters of the Sufis, for that is their place of prayer and contains fine *mehrābs*. There are always many Sufis in residence at prayer, except on Fridays when they go inside the mosque to hear the exaltation.

At the north corner of the sanctuary is a fine colonnade and a large, beautiful dome on which is inscribed: "This is the *mehrāb* of Zechariah the prophet." They say that he used to pray constantly in this place.

Along the eastern wall, in the middle of the sanctuary, is a large gateway of stone so finely hewn that one would say it has been made of a single block. It is fifty ells high and thirty wide, is carved in designs, and has two beautiful doors leading into it. Between the two doors is not more than one foot of wall space. These doors are elaborately made of iron and Damascene brass with rings and studs. They say these doors were made by Solomon son of David for his father.

Going inside through these two doors, and facing east, you find to your right two doors, one called Bāb al-Rahma [Gate of Mercy] and the other, Bāb al-Tawba [Gate of Repentance]. It is said that it was at these very doors that God accepted David's repentance. On this spot is a beautiful mosque that was once a hall but has now been made into a mosque and decorated with all sorts of carpets. It has an independent staff. Men often go there to pray and seek communion with God. For the very reason that David's repentance was accepted in that place, all people are hopeful to be forgiven their sins as well. They say that David had scarcely crossed the threshold when an inspiration came to him to the effect that God had accepted his repentance. There he remained, occupying himself with acts of obedience. I, Nāser, prayed there and asked God for grace in piety and to be cleansed of the sin of disobedience. May God the Exalted grant grace to all his servants in accordance with his pleasure and grant repentance of sin, through the sanctity of Mohammad and his pure offspring!

In the south corner of the east wall is an underground mosque, to reach which you must descend many steps. It is twenty by fifteen ells and has a stone roof supported by marble columns. It contains Jesus's cradle, which is made of stone and is large enough for men to pray in. I too prayed there. It is firmly fastened to the floor so that it cannot be moved. This is the cradle the Child Jesus was placed in when he spoke to people.[13] In this mosque the cradle takes the place of the *mehrāb*. On the east side is the *mehrāb* of Mary and another said to be that of Zachariah. The Koranic verses concerning Zachariah and Mary are inscribed in these niches, and it is said that this was Jesus' birthplace. One of the columns has the imprint of two fingers and looks as though someone had grasped it. They say that when Mary was in labor, she held onto this very column. This mosque is known as Mahd ʿIsā [Jesus' Cradle], and many brass and silver lamps are hung here and kept burning throughout the night.

Passing out through the door, again on the east wall at a corner of the large sanctuary area, you see another very beautiful mosque, twice as large as Jesus' Cradle Mosque, called al-Aqsā Mosque. This marks the spot to which God transported Moḥammad from Mecca on the night of his heavenly ascent, and thence to heaven, as is mentioned in the Koran: "Praise be unto him, who transported his servant by night, from the sacred temple of Mecca to the farther temples of Jerusalem" [Koran 17:1].

In that place is a skillfully constructed edifice with magnificent carpets and an independent staff who are always attendant. On the outside again, along the southern wall and beyond the corner, there is an uncovered courtyard about 200 ells long. The length of the mosque along the west wall is 420 ells, with the *maqsura* to the right along the south wall; it [the mosque] is 150 ells wide. It has 280 marble columns supporting a stone arcade, the tops and bottoms of which are decorated and the joints filled with lead so that the construction is extremely tight. Between every two columns is a distance of six ells, and the ground is

[13]Jesus is mentioned in the Koran (19:29f.) as having spoken from the cradle.

flagged in colored marble tile, the joints again caulked in lead. The *maqsura,* in the middle of the south wall, is large enough for sixteen columns and an enormous dome inlaid in tile, as has been described. It is filled with Maghrebi carpets, lamps, and lanterns each hung by a separate chain. There is a large *mehrāb* inlaid with tile; on either side of the niche are two marble pillars the color of red carnelian, and the whole low wall of the *maqsura* is of colored marble. To the right is Moʿāwiya's *mehrāb,* and that of Omar to the left. The ceiling is covered with wood carved in elaborate designs. Along the wall of the *maqsura* toward the courtyard are 15 gateways and ornate doors, each of which is 10 ells tall and 6 wide, 10 of them on the wall that is 420 ells long and 5 on the wall that is 150 ells long. One of these gates in particular is done in such beautifully ornate brass that one would think it was made of gold burnished with silver. It has the name of the Caliph Ma'mun on it and is said to have been sent by him from Baghdad.

When all the gates are opened, the inside of the mosque is as light as an open courtyard. However, when the wind is blowing or it is raining, the gates are closed, and then light comes from skylights. On each side of the covered portion are chests from each of the principal cities of Syria and Iraq, and *mojāwers* sit there just as they do in the Haram Mosque in Mecca.

Along the great outer wall, already described, is an arcade with forty-two arches, all the columns of which are of colored marble. This arcade joins the western one. Inside the covered portion [of the mosque] is a tank sunk into the earth such that, when covered, it is level with the floor; this is for collecting rainwater. In the south wall is a gate at the ablution pool. When anyone needs water for making ablutions, he goes there and renews his ablutions, for the mosque is so large that if you had to leave it, you would certainly miss your prayer.

The roofs are all covered with lead, and there are many tanks and cisterns sunk into the ground, since the mosque rests entirely on rock. However much it rains, no water is allowed to escape and go to waste, since it all drains into cisterns from which it can be drawn later. There are lead conduits through which the water flows. Beneath the drains are stone troughs, and in the bottom of each of these is a hole leading to a channel through which the water flows uncontaminated into the tanks. Three parasangs outside the city I saw a large reservoir in which mountain water is kept. There is a canal from there into the city mosque. Of all the city, the greatest abundance of water is found in the Friday mosque; however, in all the houses there are pools for rainwater, wherein each person collects the water from his own roof. The baths and everything else operate on rainwater as well. The cisterns in the mosque never need repair because they are made of granite, but even should there have been a crack or chink, the rock is so solidly reinforced that it never breaks. They say Solomon made all this. The tops of the cisterns look like ovens; and the well-covers, which are placed on top of every cistern lest anything fall in, are stone. The water of this city is the best and cleanest imaginable. Even when only a little rain falls, the water runs for two or three days. Even when no trace of a cloud remains in the sky, drops of rainwater continue to trickle.

I have already said that Jerusalem is built on top of a hill and that the ground is not level. The site of the mosque alone is level and even; outside the mosque, wherever the ground goes down, the wall becomes correspondingly somewhat taller, rather than having the top of the wall follow the rising and falling of the ground. At every place in the city lower than the mosque, a door has been cut to lead up to the courtyard through a tunnel. One of these doors is called Bāb al-Nabi [Prophet's Gate]. This passageway is on the *qebla* side, that is, the south, and is built so that it is ten ells wide; the height, depending on the number of steps, varies from five to twenty ells. The roof of this passageway lies under the pavement of the mosque and is strong enough for a building of such enormity to be built on top of it with no trace of strain. There are stones so enormous that the mind of man cannot comprehend how human strength could have moved them. They say this structure was made by Solomon son of David and that our Prophet Mohammad, on the night of his heavenly ascent, entered the mosque by this passage; this door indeed faces the road to Mecca. On the wall nearby is a large shield carved in stone. It is said that Hamza son of ʿAbd al-Mottaleb, the uncle of the Prophet, sat there with his shield on his back and that this is an impression of that shield.

At this gateway to the mosque, where this passageway has been constructed, is hung a double-leafed door. The outside wall at this point is nearly fifty ells high. The reason for this gate is so that the people of the quarter adjoining this end of the mosque should not have to go to another quarter when they want to enter. In the wall to the right of the door is a stone fifteen cubits high and four wide; there is no stone larger in the mosque, where there are many stones four to five ells long set at a height of thirty to forty ells in the walls.

Along the breadth of the mosque is a gate facing east called Bāb al-ʿAyn [Gate of the Spring], outside of which is a hill leading down to the Spring of Siloam. There is also another gate at ground level called Bāb al-Hetta [Gate of Forgiveness]; it is said that it was through this gate that God commanded the children of Israel to enter the mosque, as he said: "Enter into this city, and eat of the provisions thereof plentifully as ye will; and enter the gate worshiping, and say, Forgiveness! [*hetta*] we will pardon you your sins and give increase unto the well-doers" [Koran 2:58].

Yet another gate is called Bāb al-Sakīna [Gate of the Divine Presence][14] and in the adjacent vestibule is a mosque with many *mehrāb*s; the first door is kept closed so that no one can enter. They say that the Ark of the Covenant mentioned by God in the Koran was once placed there but was later borne away by the angels.

All the gates to the Jerusalem sanctuary number nine, as described.

Now I will describe the platform in the middle of the mosque courtyard, and the Rock located inside, which was the *qebla* before the emergence of Islam. The platform had to be constructed because the rock was too high to be enclosed under a roof; therefore the platform was built with the Rock as its foundation. The width is 330 cubits, the length 300 cubits, and the height 12 ells. The court is level and nicely paved with marble, and the walls, the joints of which are caulked with lead, are all four faced with marble so as to form an enclosure. The platform is so constructed that access can be gained only by specially built gangways. Going up onto the platform, you can look out over the roof of al-Aqsā Mosque. There is a cistern built below the ground to store rainwater, which runs through niches into the

[14]The name of this gate is taken from the post-Biblical concept of the *shĕkīnah*, the "aura of the presence of God" that surrounded the Ark of the Covenant. The term occurs in Koran 2:248.

cistern, and this the cleanest and best water in the entire sanctuary complex. There are four domes on the platform, the largest of which is the Qobbat al-Sakhra [Dome of the Rock], which used to be the *qebla*.

A Description of the Dome of the Rock

The mosque complex has been designed so that the platform is in the middle of the court, and the Dome of the Rock in the middle of the platform. It is an octagonal edifice, and each of the eight sides is thirty-three cubits long. There are four doors facing the cardinal points of the compass with one blank wall between each two doors. The whole wall is of masonry twenty cubits in measure. The Rock itself is one hundred ells in circumference, although it is not a perfect shape; that is, it is neither circular nor square, but a rock of irregular form like any mountain stone. On each of the four sides of the Rock is a square pier the height of the wall. Between each two square piers stands a pair of cylindrical marble pillars the same height as the piers. Resting on these twelve piers and pillars is the base of the dome, beneath which lies the Rock itself; the circumference is 120 cubits. Between the wall and these piers (as I call the square ones) and pillars (as I call the round ones hewn from one piece of stone) are six more piers of hewn stone; between each two of these are three columns of colored marble. They are equally spaced so that in the outer row there are two columns between each two piers, whereas in the inner row there are three columns between each two piers. On the capital of each pier are set four volutes, from each of which springs an arch; on the capital of each column are set two volutes so that from each column there spring two arches, whereas the capital of every pier is the spring of four arches.

The great dome rests on the twelve piers around the Rock and is so shaped that from one good parasang away the dome appears like a mountain. From the base of the dome to the top is thirty cubits. The dome sits atop the octagonal structure's straight walls twenty ells high with buttresses forming the angles of the supporting walls on top of the platform, which is itself

The Dome of the Rock of Jerusalem, viewed from the south (*qebla*) side, showing the Maqām-e Ghōri. Note that the triple stairway described by Nāṣer has been replaced. (Photographed by Felix Bonfils. From the Collections of the Harvard Semitic Museum, HSM 372.)

twelve ells high. Thus, from the ground of the sanctuary court to the summit of the dome is a total of sixty-two ells. The roof and ceiling of this structure are covered with geometric designs, and the column capitals and walls are ornate beyond description.

The Rock itself rises to the height of a man above the floor and is surrounded by a marble balustrade to keep people away. It is a bluish rock that no one has ever set foot on. On the *qebla* side is a depression that looks as though someone's foot had sunk in, as into soft clay, for even the imprint of the toes remains; there are seven such marks. What I heard is that Abraham was here, and that when Isaac was a small child he walked there and these are his footprints.

There are always people in the Dome of the Rock as *mojāwer*s and devotees. The place is nicely furnished with carpets of silk, and in the middle of the building is a silver lamp suspended over the Rock by a silver chain. There are many silver lamps here, and on each one is written its weight. They were donated by the sultan of Egypt. As I figured, there were a thousand maunds of silver. I saw one enormous candle, seven cubits long and three spans thick; it was as white as camphor and mixed with ambergris. They said that every year the sultan of Egypt sends many candles, one of which was this one, for it had the sultan's name written in gold letters around the bottom.

This place is the third most holy place of God, and it is well known among those learned in religion that prayer made in Jerusalem is worth twenty-five thousand ordinary prayers. Every prayer said in Medina is worth fifty thousand, and every prayer said Mecca is worth one hundred thousand. May God grant to all his servants success in attaining this!

I have already stated that all the roofs and domes are covered with lead and that on each of the four sides of the structure is a large double door made of teak. These doors are always kept shut.

Next to this structure is another dome called Qobbat al-Selsela [the Dome of the Chain], which is where David hung the chain that could not be reached by anyone other than the innocent, for the guilty and unjust could never pull it. This is well known to the learned.[15] That dome rests on eight marble columns and

[15]For the legend of David's chain of justice, see al-Kesā'i, *Tales of the Prophets of al-Kisa'i*, tr. W. M. Thackston, Jr. (Boston: Twayne, 1978), pp. 286–288.

six stone piers, and it is open on all sides except the *qebla* direction, which is walled up and has a beautiful *mehrāb.*

Also on the platform is another dome, which rests on four marble columns; it too is walled on the *qebla* side and has a fine *mehrāb*. This is called Gabriel's Dome. There are no carpets in this dome, the ground being paved with flat slabs of rock. They say that on the night of the Prophet's heavenly ascent, the Borāq was brought here for the Prophet to mount.[16]

Twenty cubits away from Gabriel's Dome is another dome called the Prophet's Dome. This too rests on four marble piers.

They say that on the night of the heavenly ascent, the Prophet first prayed in the Dome of the Rock and placed his hand on the Rock. When he had come out, the Rock rose up because of his majesty. He put his hand on the Rock, and it froze in its place, half of it being still suspended in the air. From there the Prophet came to the dome that is attributed to him and mounted the Borāq, for which reason that dome is so venerated. Beneath the Rock is a large cave where candles are kept burning. They say that when the Rock moved to rise up, this space was left, and, when it froze, this cave remained.

A Description of the Stairways Leading to the Platform

There are six stairways up to the platform, each of which has a name. From the *qebla* side are two ways up the platform. Standing at a point along one side of the platform, one sees a set of stairs to the right and another to the left. The one to the right is called Maqām al-Nabi [the Prophet's Station]; the one to the left, Maqām-e Ghōri [the Ghorid Station]. The Prophet's Station is so called because the Prophet mounted the platform by these stairs and thence into the Dome of the Rock. The road to the Hejaz is indeed on that side. Now these stairs are twenty cubits broad and are made of hewn stone, each step being one or two slabs of square-hewn stone. They are so arranged that they can be scaled on horseback. At the top of the stairs are four piers of a green marble that resembles emerald, except that the marble has many

[16]The Borāq is the heavenly animal upon which the Prophet ascended into heaven. In late medieval iconography the Borāq is a winged horse with a human female head.

different colored flecks in it. Each column is ten cubits tall and so thick that only with difficulty could two men reach around it. Atop these four columns rise three arches placed so that the middle one is directly opposite the steps. The top of the arcade is flat, with a gallery and crenellations above so that the whole looks squared off. The pillars and arches are covered with gold and enamel designs and are too beautiful to describe. The balustrades around the platform are all of a flecked green marble that looks like a meadow with flowers in bloom.

The Ghorid Station stairway consists of a triple flight, that is, a middle stairway directly opposite the platform flanked on either side by stairways, so that people can go up by any one of three different ways. Here too are similar columns, arches, and a gallery made, as I have already said, of hewn stone. Each step is of two or three long slabs. Across the arcade is inscribed in gold and fine calligraphy, "By the order of Prince Layth al-Dawla Nushtakin the Ghorid." They say that this Layth al-Dawla was a slave of the sultan of Egypt and that he had these stairs and gangways built.

On the west side of the platform there are also two stairways all as elaborately constructed as what I have already described. On the east side is only one stair, likewise elaborate, with columns, arches, and crenellations. This is called Maqām Sharqi [Eastern Station]. On the north side is another approach, higher and broader than the others, but also with columns and arches. It is called Maqām Shāmi [Syrian Station]. I reckoned that a hundred thousand dinars must have been spent on these six stairways and approaches.

Toward the north side of the courtyard of the Sanctuary, but not on the platform, is something like a small mosque surrounded by a masonry enclosure. Its walls are no[17] higher than a man, and it is called Mehrāb Dā'ud [David's Oratory]. Nearby the enclosure is a rock about as tall as a man, the top of which is no larger than what could be covered by a small rug. It is a rough stone and is said to have been Solomon's footstool. They say that Solomon sat there while the Sanctuary was being built.

This much I saw and sketched myself inside the Jerusalem Sanctuary, and I made notes in a diary I had with me right

[17]Read, with Tehran edition, *nabāshad* for Dabir-Siyāqi's *bāshad*.

there. Among the strange things I saw in the Jerusalem Sanctuary was a walnut tree.

I then decided to make a visit to the tomb of Abraham, the Friend of God. On Wednesday the first of Dhu'l-Qaʿda 438 [29 April 1047] I set out for my destination. From Jerusalem to the shrine is six parasangs to the south. Along the way are many villages and much cultivation and orchards of trees that need no irrigation, such as grapes, figs, olives, wild[18] sumac, and so forth. Two parasangs outside the city is a cluster of four villages where there is a spring and also many gardens and orchards. It is called "Paradise" because it is such a nice spot. One parasang outside Jerusalem the Christians have a place they hold in great veneration, and there are always many pilgrims and people holding retreat there. It is called Bethlehem, and the Christians, many from Byzantium, make sacrifices there. I spent my first night out from the city in that place.

A Description of the Shrine of Abraham at Hebron

The people of Syria and Jerusalem call this shrine Khalil [Hebron],[19] whereas the proper name of the village, which they do not use, is Matlun. The shrine is endowed with many villages in addition to this one. The village has a spring that flows from rock. Not much water comes from it, and it is a long way off, but a channel has been dug to bring the water to just outside the village, where a covered cistern has been constructed to store the water lest it go to waste and so that there will be enough for the people of the village and also for the pilgrims who come there. The shrine itself is on the south side of the village, to the southeast. There are four masonry walls eighty cubits long, forty cubits wide, and twenty cubits high. The top of each wall is two cubits thick. There is a *mehrāb* and a *maqsura* along the width of the structure, and in the *maqsura* are fine *mehrābs* and two tombs placed so that the heads are toward the *qebla*. Each one is carved

[18]Read, with Tehran and Berlin editions, *khwadrōy* for Dabir-Siyāqi's *khwad.*

[19]Hebron, where the Shrine of Abraham is located, is known in Arabic as al-Khalil, after Abraham's epithet, *Khalil Allāh* ("Friend of God"); see 2 Chronicles 20:7.

from stone and is about as long as a man. The one to the right is the tomb of Isaac, son of Abraham, and the other is his wife's. The distance between the two is ten ells. Inside this shrine the floor and walls are decorated with costly rugs and Maghrebi carpets even finer than brocade. I saw a prayer carpet said to have been sent by a prince of the army who was a slave of the sultan of Egypt. He was supposed to have bought it in Egypt for thirty gold dinars, which is more than he would have paid for Byzantine brocade. I never saw its equal anywhere. Coming out of the *maqsura* into the shrine courtyard, you see two structures opposite the *qebla:* the one to the right is a large building that contains the tomb of Abraham, the Friend of God. Inside there is another structure that you cannot walk all the way around, but it has four small windows through which visitors can look and see the tomb as they walk about. The whole structure is covered with brocade hangings from floor to ceiling, and the tomb is three ells long. Many lamps and silver lampholders are suspended therein. The other monument, to the left of the *qebla*, contains the tomb of Sarah, Abraham's wife. Between these two structures is a vestibule-like passageway containing the doors to the two small monuments. Here also are hung many lamps and lampholders. Coming out of these two houses, you see two more mausolea: the one on the right contains the remains of the Prophet Jacob, and the one to the left, those of his wife. Next to these are buildings that were Abraham's guesthouses. Altogether there are six tombs in this shrine.

Outside these four walls is a hill where the tomb of Joseph son of Jacob is located under a nicely built dome with a stone tomb. On the side where the ground is level, beyond Joseph's Dome and the shrine, is a large cemetery to which bodies have been brought for interment from all parts. On the roof of the *maqsura* inside the shrine are cells to house guests who stop there. The place is heavily endowed with villages and freeholding in Jerusalem. Most of the crop is barley, wheat being less cultivated; there are, of course, many olives. Visitors, guests, and travelers are given bread and olives. There are also many gristmills where oxen and mules grind flour all day long. There are also young girls who bake bread every day, each loaf weighing one maund. Everyone who goes there is given a daily ration of one loaf of bread, a bowl of lentils cooked with olive oil, and raisins, a custom that has been maintained from the time of Abraham himself down to the present. On some days there are five hundred people present, all of whom receive this hospitality. They say that a long time ago, before this shrine was built, no one could enter and that the visit had to be made from outside. Then, when the Mahdi was established in the land of Egypt, he ordered the structure opened up. Many utensils, hangings, and carpets were placed therein and major reparations were made inside the shrine. The entrance is in the middle of the north wall and is four ells above the ground. On either side are stone steps leading up on one side and down on the other. There is a small iron door mounted there.

From there I returned to Jerusalem and then set out on foot with a group of people heading for the Hejaz. Our guide was a strong, pleasant-featured man who went on foot and was called Abu Bakr Hamadāni. The middle of Dhu 'l-Qaʿda 438 [May 1047] I departed from Jerusalem. After three days we came to a place called ʿArʿar, where there were gardens with running water. We then came to another stopping place called Wādi al-Qorā. After that we stopped in one more place and in ten days reached Mecca.

That year there were no caravans from anywhere, and foodstuffs were not to be found. We stopped in the Druggists' Lane just opposite the Prophet's Gate. On Monday we were at ʿArafāt, although the people were in danger of marauding Arabs. Returning from ʿArafāt, we stayed two days in Mecca and then set out again for Syria and Jerusalem.

On the 5th of Moharram 439 [2 July 1047] we arrived in Jerusalem. I have not detailed anything of Mecca and the Pilgrimage here because I will describe it all under my last Pilgrimage.

The Christians have a church in Jerusalem called Bayʿat al-Qomāma [Church of the Resurrection], which they hold in particular veneration. Every year many people come from Byzantium to visit it, and the Byzantine king himself comes in disguise so that no one will recognize him. In the days when the ruler of Egypt was al-Hākem be-Amr Allāh, the Byzantine emperor came. al-Hākem found out about it and said to one of his equerries, "In the mosque of Jerusalem a man of such-and-such a description wearing such-and-such clothes will be seated. Go to him and say that al-Hākem has sent you. Tell him not to imagine that I have no knowledge of his presence and not to fear, for I have no ill intent with regard to him." It was this very al-Hākem who ordered this church plundered and pulled down, and it remained in this state of ruination for a time. Afterwards the emperor sent emissaries with many gifts to seek a reconciliation and to intercede for permission to rebuild the church. It is large enough to hold eight thousand people inside and is extremely ornate, with colored marble and designs and pictures. It is arrayed with Byzantine brocades and is painted. Much gold has been used, and in several places there are pictures of Jesus riding on an ass and also pictures of other prophets such as Abraham, Ishmael, Isaac, and Jacob and his sons, which are varnished in oil of sandarac and covered with fine, transparent glass that does not block any of the painting. This they have done so that dust and dirt cannot harm the pictures, and every day servants clean the glass. There are several other places just as elaborate, but it would take too long to describe them. There is one place in this church painted in two parts to represent heaven and hell and their inhabitants; in all the world there is nothing to equal it. Many priests and monks remain here to read the Gospel, pray, and occupy themselves with acts of devotion all day and night.

Journey to Egypt

After Jerusalem I decided to voyage to Egypt by sea and thence again to Mecca. As there was such an adverse wind that the ship could not set out to sea, I therefore proceeded by land. Passing through Ramla, I came to a town on the edge of the sea called Ascalon, which had a fine bazaar and cathedral mosque. I saw an old arch said to have been at one time [part of] a mosque. It was of stone and so huge that it would have cost a great deal to pull it down. Beyond there I saw many villages and towns that would take too long to describe fully.

Shortly, I arrived at a port called Tina, from which you proceed to Tennis. I boarded a boat and sailed over to Tennis, which is on an island. It is a pleasant city and so far from the mainland that you cannot even see the shore from rooftops. The city is populous and has good bazaars and two cathedral mosques. I estimated there were ten thousand shops, a hundred of which were pharmacies. In the summer they sell *kashkāb* in the market, since it is a tropical climate and people suffer so from the heat.

They weave multicolored linen for turbans, bandages, and women's clothing. The colored linen of Tennis is unequaled anywhere except by the white linen woven in Damietta. That which is woven in the royal workshop is not sold to anyone. I heard that the king of Fārs once sent twenty thousand dinars to Tennis to buy one suit of clothing of their special material. [His agents] stayed there for several years but were unsuccessful in obtaining any. What the weavers are most famous for is their "special" material. I heard that someone there had woven a turban for the sultan of Egypt that cost five hundred gold dinars. I saw the turban myself and was told it was worth four thousand dinars. In this city of Tennis they weave [a type of cloth called] *buqalamun*, which is found nowhere else in the world. It is an iridescent cloth that appears of different hues at different times of the day. It is exported east and west from Tennis. I heard that the ruler of Byzantium once sent a message to the sultan of Egypt that he would exchange a hundred cities of his realm of Tennis alone. The sultan did not accept, of course, knowing that what he wanted with this city was its linen and *buqalamun*.

When the water of the Nile rises, it pushes the salt water of the sea away from Tennīs so that the water is fresh for ten parasangs. For that time of the year large, reinforced, underground cisterns called *masnaʿas* have been constructed on the island. When the Nile water forces the salty seawater back, they fill these cisterns by opening a watercourse from the sea into them, and the city exists for a whole year on this supply. When anyone has an excess of water, he will sell to others, and there are also endowed *masnaʿas* from which water is given out to foreigners.

The population of this city is fifty thousand, and there are at any given time at least a thousand ships at anchor belonging both to private merchants and to the sultan; since nothing is there, everything that is consumed must be brought in from the outside. All external transactions with the island are made therefore by ship, and there is a fully armed garrison stationed there as a precaution against attack by Franks and Byzantines. I heard from reliable sources that one thousand dinars a day go from there into the sultan's treasury. Everyday the people of the city turn that amount over to the tax collector, and he in turn remits it to the treasury before it shows a deficit. Nothing is taken from anyone by force. The full price is paid for all the linen and *buqalamun* woven for the sultan, so that the people work willingly—not as in some other countries, where the artisans are forced to labor for the vizier and sultan! They weave covers for camel litters and striped saddle-cloths for the aristocrats; in return, they import fruits and foodstuffs from the Egyptian countryside.

They also make superior iron tools such as shears, knives, and so on. I saw a pair of shears imported from there to Egypt and selling for five dinars. They were made so that when the pin was taken out, the shears came apart, and when the pin was replaced they worked again.

In that locale women are afflicted at times with a peculiar illness that causes them to cry out two or three times like an epileptic, after which they regain their senses. In Khorasan I had heard that there was an island where the women cry like cats, which is similar to what I have just described. From Tennis to Constantinople it is a twenty-day voyage by ship.

We set out for Egypt. When we reached the seashore, we found a boat going up the Nile. As the Nile nears the coast, it splits into many branches and flows fragmented into the sea. The branch we were on is called Rumesh. The boat sailed along until we came to a town called Sālehiyya, which is very fertile. Many ships capable of carrying up to two hundred *kharvār*s of commodities for sale in the groceries of Cairo are made there. Were it not done in that manner, it would be impossible to bring provisions into the city by animal with such efficiency. We disembarked at Sālehiyya and proceeded that very night to the city.

On Sunday the 7th of Safar 439 [3 August 1047], which was Ormozd Day of Shahrivār, old reckoning, we were in Cairo.

A Description of Cairo and the Provinces

The River Nile flows from the southwest, through the city of Cairo, and on into the Mediterranean Sea. When the Nile floods, it swells to twice the size of the Oxus at Termedh. The water flows through Nubia before reaching Egypt. The province of Nubia is mountainous, while Egypt lies on the plain. The first place one comes to in Egypt from Nubia is Aswan, three hundred parasangs from Cairo. All the town and provincial seats are on the banks of the river, and that region is called Upper Egypt. When ships reach Aswan, they can go no further because the water passes through narrow defiles and turns into rapids.

Farther upriver to the south is the province of Nubia, which is ruled by another king. The people there are black, and their religion is Christianity. Traders go there taking beads, combs, and trinkets and bring back slaves to Egypt, where the slaves are either Nubian or Greek. I saw wheat and millet from Nubia, both of which were black.

They say that no one has been able to ascertain the source of the Nile, and I heard that the sultan of Egypt sent some people who went along the Nile banks for a year investigating but were unable to discover the source. It is said, however, that it comes from a mountain in the south called Jabal al-Qamar [Mountain of the Moon].

When the sun enters Cancer, the Nile begins its increase and gradually rises day by day to twenty cubits above its winter level. In the city of Old Cairo measuring devices have been constructed, and there is an agent who receives a salary of one thousand dinars to watch and see how much the level rises. From the day it begins its increase, criers are sent through the city to proclaim how many "fingers" God has increased the Nile that day. When it has risen one ell, the good news is heralded and public rejoicing proclaimed until it reaches eighteen cubits, the normal increase. Less than this is considered a deficiency, and alms are distributed, holy intentions vowed, and general sorrow ensues. More is a cause for celebration and rejoicing. Unless the level goes above eighteen cubits, the sultan's land tax is not levied on the peasantry.

Water channels with smaller canals branching off have been dug from the Nile in all directions, and the villages of the countryside are situated along them. There are so many waterwheels that it would be difficult to count them. All country villages in Egypt are built on high places and hills because when the Nile floods the whole land is inundated. So that they will be flooded, the villages are thus placed on higher ground. People normally travel from village to village by boat, and from one end of the realm to the other they have constructed earthen dikes, along the top of which you can walk beside the river. That structure is repaired yearly by an expert at a cost of ten thousand dinars to the sultan's treasury. The people of the countryside make all necessary preparations for the four months their land is beneath the water, and everyone bakes and dries enough bread to last these four months without spoiling.

The water usually rises for forty days until it has risen eighteen cubits. Then it remains at that level for another forty days, neither increasing nor decreasing. Thereupon it gradually decreases for another forty days until it reaches the winter level. When the water begins to recede, the people follow it down, planting as the land is left dry. All their agriculture, both winter and summer, follows this pattern. They need no other source of water.

The city of Cairo lies between the Nile and the sea, the Nile flowing from south to north into the sea. From Cairo to Alexandria is thirty parasangs, and Alexandria is on the shore of the Mediterranean and the banks of the Nile. From there much fruit is brought to Cairo by boat. There is a lighthouse that I saw in Alexandria, on top of which used to be an incendiary mirror. Whenever a ship came from Istanbul and approached opposite the mirror, fire would fall from the mirror and burn the ship up. The Byzantines exerted great effort and employed all manner of subterfuge, until they finally sent someone who broke the mirror. In the days of al-Hākem, the sultan of Egypt, a man appeared who was willing to fix the mirror as it had once been, but al-Hākem said it was not necessary, that the situation was well under control, since at that time the Greeks sent gold and goods in tribute and were content for the armies of Egypt not to go near them.

Alexandria's drinking water comes from rain, and all over the plain of Alexandria are those fallen stone columns previously described. The sea extends to Qayrawān, which is 150 parasangs from Egypt. The largest city of the Qayrawān region is Sejelmāsa, which is 4 parasangs from the sea. It is a large city, situated in the desert, with strong walls. Next to it is al-Mahdiyya, which was built by al-Mahdi, a descendant of Prince of the Faithful Hosayn son of ʿAli, after he took the Maghreb and Andalusia, which, as of this date, are in the hands of the sultan of Egypt. It snows there but never enough to cover the feet. To the right of Andalusia the sea opens out to the north. From Egypt to Andalusia is one thousand parasangs, and it is all Muslim. Andalusia is a large and mountainous province where it snows and freezes; the people have white skin and red hair. Most of them have cat-eyes like the Slavs. It is "under" the Mediterranean, since from their point of view the sea is to the east. Turning right at Andalusia and going north, the shore eventually joins Byzantium. Many go on raids to Byzantium; if they like they can go by ship to Constantinople, but there are many gulfs, each of which is two to three hundred parasangs wide and cannot be crossed except by ship or ferry. I heard repeatedly from reliable men that the circumference of this sea is four thousand parasangs and that one branch of the sea leads to the Darkness, for they say that the head of that inlet is perpetually frozen because the sun never reaches there. One of the islands in this sea is Sicily, which can be reached from Egypt in twenty days. There are also many other islands. It is said that Sicily is eighty parasangs square and belongs to the sultan of Egypt. Every year a ship goes and brings tribute to Egypt. They bring very fine linen and striped stuff from there, one piece of which is worth ten dinars in Egypt.

Going east from Egypt, you reach the Red Sea. The city of Qolzom is located on the shore of this sea and is thirty parasangs from Cairo. This sea is a gulf of the ocean that splits off at Aden to the north and ends at Qolzom. The width of this gulf is said to be two hundred parasangs. Between Cairo and the gulf is mountain and desert where there is neither water nor growth. Whoever wants to go to Mecca from Egypt must go east. From Qolzom there are two ways, one by land and one by sea. The land route can be traversed in fifteen days, but it is all desert and three hundred parasangs long. Most of the caravans from Egypt take that way. By sea it takes twenty days to reach al-Jār, a small town in the Hejaz on the sea. From al-Jār to Medina it takes three days. From Medina to Mecca is one hundred parasangs. Following the coastline from al-Jār, you will come to the Yemen and the coast of Aden; continuing in that direction, you will eventually wind up in India and China. Continuing southward from Aden and slightly westward, you will come to Zanzibar and

Ethiopia, which will be described presently. Going south from Egypt through Nubia, you come to the province of the Masmudis, which is a land of broad pasture lands, many animals, and heavyset, strong-limbed, squat, black-skinned men; there are many soldiers of this sort in Egypt, with hideous faces and huge bodies. They are called Masmudis and fight as infantry with swords and spears, as they are incapable of wielding any other weapons.

A Description of the City of Cairo

Coming south from Syria, the first city one encounters is (New) Cairo, Old Cairo being situated farther south. Cairo is called al-Qāhera al-Moʿezziyya, and the garrison town is called Fostāt. This came about because al-Moʿezz le-Din Allāh, one of the descendents of the Prince of the Faithful Ḥosayn son of ʿAli, having conquered the Maghreb up to Andalusia, sent his army from the Maghreb in the direction of Egypt. To reach there, they had to cross the Nile, which is impassable for two reasons: first, the river is too broad, and second, there are so many crocodiles that any animal falling into the water is immediately devoured. Then, on the outskirts of the city of Cairo, they put a talisman on the road so that no men or animals would be harmed, but no one dares to enter the water any place other than there within an arrowshot of the city. Then al-Moʿezz le-Din Allāh sent his armies to the spot where Cairo is today, ordering them to send a black dog into the water ahead of them so they could follow without fear. It is said there were on that day thirty thousand cavalrymen, all his slaves. And the black dog went in ahead of the army, which followed behind across the water without a single creature harmed. There is no indication that anyone had crossed the Nile on horseback before this incident, which occurred in 358 [A.D. 969]. The sultan himself came by ship, and the boats in which he arrived were emptied near Cairo, brought out of the water, and left abandoned on the dry land. The man who told me this tale saw these boats himself, seven of them, each 150 cubits long and 70 cubits wide. They had remained there untouched for eighty years, as it was the year 441 [A.D. 1049] when he reached the spot.

When al-Moʿezz le-Din Allāh came to Egypt, the commander-in-chief from the caliph in Baghdad surrendered to him, and al-Moʿezz came with his forces to the place that is now New Cairo. He named his army camp al-Qāhera ("Victoria") since his army had gained victory there. He ordered that none of his soldiers should enter the city or go into anyone's house. In the desert he ordered a garrison built, and he commanded his retinue to lay the foundations for houses and buildings, which in time became a city whose equal is hardly to be found.

I estimated that there were no less than twenty thousand shops in Cairo, all of which belong to the sultan. Many shops are rented for as much as ten dinars a month, and none for less than two. There is no end of caravanserais, bathhouses and other public buildings—all property of the sultan, for no one owns any property except houses and what he himself builds. I heard that in Cairo and Old Cairo there are eight thousand buildings belonging to the sultan that are leased out, with the rent collected monthly. These are leased and rented to people on tenancy-at-will, and no sort of coercion is employed.

The sultan's palace is in the middle of Cairo and is encompassed by an open space so that no building abuts it. Engineers who have measured it have found it to be the size of Mayyāfāreqin. As the ground is open all around it, every night there are a thousand watchmen, five hundred mounted and five hundred on foot, who blow trumpets and beat drums at the time of evening prayer and then patrol until daybreak. Viewed from outside the city, the sultan's palace looks like a mountain because of all the different buildings and the great height. From inside the city, however, one can see nothing at all because the walls are so high. They say that twelve thousand hired servants work in this palace, in addition to the women and slavegirls, whose number no one knows. It is said, nonetheless, that there are thirty thousand individuals in the palace, which consists of twelve buildings. The harem has ten gates on the ground level, each with a name, as follows (excluding the subterranean ones): Bāb al-Dhahab, Bāb al-Bahr, Bāb al-Rih, Bāb al-Zahuma, Bāb al-Salām, Bāb al-Zabarjad, Bāb al-ʿId, Bāb al-Fotuh, Bāb al-Zallāqa, and Bāb al-Sariyya[?].[20] There is a subterranean entrance through which

[20]Of these gates, the following are in conformity with the palace gates as they are known from other medieval and modern sources: Bāb al-Dhahab [Golden Gate], Bāb al-Baḥr [River Gate], Bāb al-Riḥ [Wind Gate, reading *riḥ* for Dabir-

the sultan may pass on horseback. Outside the city he has built another palace connected to the harem palace by a passageway with a reinforced ceiling. The walls of this palace are of rocks hewn to look like one piece of stone, and there are belvederes and tall porticos. Inside the vestibule are platforms for the ministers of state; servants are blacks and Greeks. The grand vizier is a personnage exceptional in his asceticism, piety, trustworthiness, truthfulness, learning, and intellect. The custom of wine-drinking has never been permitted there, that is, in the days of al-Hākem, under whose reign also no woman was allowed outside her own house and no one made raisins, as a precaution against making intoxicating beverages. No one dares to drink wine. Beer is not drunk either since it is said to be intoxicating, and thus forbidden.

A Description of the City of New Cairo

The city of New Cairo has five gates, Bāb al-Nasr. Bāb al-Fotuh, Bāb al-Qantara, Bāb al-Zowayla, and Bāb al-Khalij. There is no wall, but the buildings are even stronger and higher than ramparts, and every house and building is itself a fortress. Most of the buildings are five stories tall, although some are six. Drinking water is from the Nile, and water carriers transport water by camel. The closer the well is to the river, the sweeter the well water; it becomes more brackish the farther you get from the Nile. Old and New Cairo are said to have fifty thousand camels belonging to water carriers. The water carriers who port water on their backs are separate: they have brass cups and jugs and go into the narrow lanes where a camel cannot pass.

Siyāqi's edition *sarij*], Bāb al-Zahuma, Bāb al-Zabarjad [Emerald Gate] (usually known as Bāb al-Zomorrod; apparently Nāṣer or a later scribe has inserted the Persian word *zabarjad* for the Arabic *zomorrod*, both of which mean "emerald"), Bāb al-ʿId [Festival Gate]. Bāb al-Fotuh [Fate of Conquest] is one of the city gates; the Bāb al-Zallāqa was named for a ramp leading up to the gate. Bāb al-Salām [Gate of Peace] and Bāb al-Sariyya (?, perhaps a scribal error for Bāb al-Torba [Tomb Gate]) have not been identified. See K. A. C. Creswell, *The Muslim Architecture of Egypt* (New York: Hacket Art Books, 1978), pp. 33ff. and Paul Ravaisse, "Essai sur l'histoire et sur la topographie du Caire," *MMAFC*, vol. 1, pp. 421ff.

In the midst of the houses in the city are gardens and orchards watered by wells. In the sultan's harem are the most beautiful gardens imaginable. Waterwheels have been constructed to irrigate these gardens. There are trees planted and pleasure parks built even on the roofs. At the time I was there, a house on a lot twenty by twelve ells was being rented for fifteen dinars a month. The house was four stories tall, three of which were rented out. The tenant wanted to take the topmost floor also for [an additional] five dinars, but the landlord would not give it to him, saying that he might want to go there sometimes, although, during the year we were there, he did not come twice. These houses are so magnificent and fine that you would think they were made of jewels, not of plaster, tile, and stone! All the houses of Cairo are built separate one from another, so that no one's trees or outbuildings are against anyone else's walls. Thus, whenever anyone needs to, he can open the walls of his house and add on, since it causes no detriment to anyone else.

Going west outside the city, you find a large canal called al-Khalij [Canal], which was built by the father of the present sultan, who has three hundred villages on his private property along the canal. The canal was cut from Old to New Cairo, where it turns and runs past the sultan's palace. Two kiosks are built at the head of the canal, one called Lulu [Pearl] and the other Jawhara [Jewel].

Cairo has four cathedral mosques where men pray on Fridays. One of these is called al-Azhar, another al-Nūr, another the Mosque of al-Hākem, and the fourth the Mosque of al-Moʿezz. This last mosque is outside the city on the banks of the Nile. When you face the *qebla* in Egypt, you have to turn toward the ascent of Aries. The distance between Old and New Cairo is less than a mile, Old Cairo being to the south and New Cairo to the north. The Nile flows through Old Cairo and reaches New Cairo, and the orchards and outbuildings of the two cities overlap. During the summer, when the plain and lowlands are inundated, only the sultan's garden, which is on a promontory and consequently not flooded, remains dry.

A Description of the Opening of the Canal

When the Nile is increasing, that is, from the tenth of Shahrivar until the thirtieth of Ābān, with its level rising eighteen ells above the winter level, the heads of the canals and channels are closed throughout the land. Then the canal called al-Khalij, which begins in Old Cairo and passes through New Cairo, and which is the sultan's personal property, is opened with the sultan in attendance. Afterwards, all the other canals and channels are opened throughout the countryside. This day is one of the biggest festivals of the year and is called Rokūb Fath al-Khalij ("riding forth to open the canal"). When the season approaches, a large pavilion of Byzantine brocade spun with gold and set with gems, large enough for a hundred horsemen to stand in its shade, is elaborately assembled at the head of the canal for the sultan. In front of this canopy are set up a striped tent and another large pavilion. Three days before the Rokub, drums are beat and trumpets sounded in the royal stables so that the horses will get accustomed to the sound. When the sultan mounts, ten thousand horses with gold saddles and bridles and jewel-studded reins stand at rest all of them with saddle-cloths of Byzantine brocade and *buqalamun* woven seamless to order. In the borders of the cloth are woven inscriptions bearing the name of the sultan of Egypt. On each horse is a spear or coat of armor and a helmet on the pommel, along with every other type of weapon. There are also many camels and mules with handsome panniers and howdahs, all studded with gold and jewels. Their coverings are sewn with pearls.

Were I to describe everything about this day of [the opening of] the canal, it would take too long.

The sultan's soldiers stand in groups and battalions, and each ethnic group has a name.[21] One group is called the Kotāmis,

[21]The Kotāmis were Berbers of the Kotāma tribe who were successfully converted to Ismailism by the missionary activity of Abu ʿAbd Allāh al-Shiʿi, who paved the way for the declaration of ʿObayd Allāh as *mahdi* and caliph (see EI^2, II, 852). The Bāṭelis were also of North African origin and had a quarter near the Bāb al-Zowayla. The Masmudis were of the al-Maṣmuda, a North African tribe (see Yāqut, IV, 544); after "Maṣāmeda" in the text, read, with the Tehran edition, *sepāhiyān* "infantry soldiers" for Dabir-Siyāqi's edition *siyāhān* "blacks"). The Mashāreqa, or *mashreqis* ("easterners"), were mainly Daylamite soldiery. The

and they came from Qayrawān under al-Moʿezz le-Din Allāh and are said to number twenty thousand horsemen. Another group called the Bātelis came from the Maghreb before the sultan came to Egypt; they are said to be fifteen thousand horsemen in number. Another group, the Masāmeda, are infantry soldiers from the lands of the Masmūdīs and number twenty thousand. Another group, called the Mashāreqa [Easterners], are Turks and Persians, non-Arab by origin; although most of them were born in Egypt, their name derives from their place of origin, and they number ten thousand powefully built men. Another group is called ʿAbid al-Sherā, slaves who have been purchased; they are said to be thirty thousand in number. Yet another group are called the "Bedouins," originating from the Hejaz, and all fifty thousand of them carry spears. Another group, called Ostādhs, are servants, both white and black, and were bought for service; they number thirty thousand horsemen. Another group numbering ten thousand, who originate from all over the world and are just foot soldiers, are called Sarā'is: they have a separate commander-in-chief, and each ethnic group uses its own type of weaponry. Another group are called Zanjis, thirty thousand in number; they fight with swords only. All of these soldiers are on the sultan's pay, and each receives a fixed salary and/or wage according to his rank. Never has a draft been written against any tax collector or peasant; rather, the tax collectors annually remit the taxes of each province to the central treasury, and at stipulated intervals the army's pay is disbursed. Hence, no governmental agent or peasant is ever troubled by demands from the army.

There is also a contingent of princes from all over the world—the Maghreb, the Yemen, Byzantium, Slavia, Nubia, and Abyssinia—who have come here but who are not reckoned in the ranks of the regular army. The sons of the Chosroes of Daylam and their mother have also come here, and the sons of Georgian kings, Daylamite princes, the sons of the khaqan of Turkistan, and people of other ranks and stations, such as schol-

ʿAbid al-sherā were Nubians who had been purchased as slaves, as their name indicates. Ostādhs ("masters"), as Nāṣer notes, were purchased military slaves. "Sarā'i", if the term is correct, derives from *sarā* ("palace, royal building"). The Zanjis (plural *zonuj*) were Blacks.

ars, literati, poets, and jurisprudents, all of whom have fixed stipends. No aristocrat receives less than five hundred dinars, some drawing stipends of up to two thousand dinars. The only function they have to perform is to make a salaam to the grand vizier, when he sits in state, and then withdraw to their places.

But let us return to our account of the opening of the canal. On the morning when the sultan is going out for the ceremony, ten thousand men are hired to hold the steeds we have already described. These parade by the hundred, preceded by bugles, drums, and clarions and followed by army battalions, from the Harem Gate up to the head of the canal. Each of these hirelings who holds a horse is given three dirhems. Next come horses and camels fitted with litters and caparisons, and following these come camels bearing howdahs. At some distance behind all of these comes the sultan, a well-built, clean-shaven youth with cropped hair, a descendant of Hosayn son of ʿAli. He is mounted on a camel with plain saddle and bridle with no gold or silver and wears a white shirt, as is the custom in Arab countries, with a wide cummerbund, which is called *dorrāʿ* in Persia but *dabiqi* in Egypt. The value of this alone is said to be ten thousand dinars. On his head he has a turban of the same color, and in his hand he holds a large, very costly whip. Before him walk three hundred Daylamites wearing Byzantine goldspun cloth with cummerbunds and wide sleeves, as is the fashion in Egypt. They all carry spears and arrows and wear leggings. At the sultan's side rides a parasol-bearer with a bejewelled, gold turban and a suit of clothing worth ten thousand dinars. The parasol he holds is extremely ornate and studded with jewels and pearls. No other rider accompanies the sultan, but he is preceded by Daylamites. To his left and right are thurifers burning ambergris and aloe. The custom here is for the people to prostrate themselves and say a prayer as the sultan passes. After the sultan comes the grand vizier with the chief justice and a large contingent of religious and governmental officials.

The sultan proceeds to the head of the canal, where court has been set up, and remains mounted beneath the pavilion for a time. He is then handed a spear, which he throws at the dam. Men quickly set to work with picks and shovels to demolish the dam, and the water, which has built up on the other side, breaks through and floods the canal.

On this day the whole population of Old and New Cairo

comes to witness the spectacle of the opening of the canal and to see all sorts of wonderful sporting events. The first ship that sails into the canal is filled with deaf-mutes, whom they must consider auspicious. On that day the sultan distributes alms to these people.

There are twenty-one boats belonging to the sultan, which are usually kept tied up like animals in a stable, in an artificial lake the size of two or three playing fields next to the sultan's palace; each boat is fifty yards long and twenty wide and is so ornate with gold, silver, jewels, and brocade that were I to describe them I could fill many pages.

The sultan also has a garden called ʿAyn al-Shams two parasangs outside the city: there is a freshwater spring after which the garden, said to have been Pharaoh's, was named. Near the garden I saw an ancient edifice made of four large stones, each of which was thirty ells tall and shaped like a minaret. From the top of each of these water trickles, but no one knew what it used to be.

There is a balsam tree in the garden, and it is said that the ancestors of the present sultan brought the seeds of this tree from the Maghreb and planted them and that in all the world there is no other like it, not even in the Maghreb. Although many seeds are produced, they will not grow just anywhere, and even when a tree does grow elsewhere, it does not produce oil. The tree itself looks like a myrtle tree. When it reaches maturity, the branches are scored, and cups are attached to catch the sap-like oil that comes out. When the oil is completely drained, the tree dries up, and the gardeners take the wood to town to sell. It has a thick bark that, when stripped, tastes like almond. The next year branches again sprout from the roots, and the process can be repeated.

There are in the city of Cairo ten quarters, which they call as follows: Barjawān, Zowayla, al-Jawdariyya, al-Omarā, al-Dayālema, al-Rum, al-Bāteliyya, Qasr-al-Shawk, ʿAbid al-Sherā, and al-Masāmeda.[22].

[22]The quarter names that have special significance are: al-Omarā [Emirs, or Commanders], al-Dayālema [the Daylamites], al-Rum [the Greeks], al-Bāṭeliyya [the Bāṭeli soldiers, see previous note], ʿAbid al-sherā [purchased slaves], and Maṣāmeda [the Maṣmudis, see previous note]. Some of these quarters survived as quarters until later times; see al-Maqrizi, *Ketāb al-kheṭaṭ al maqriziyya* (al-Shiyāḥ: Eḥyā' al-ʿOlum, n.d.), vol. 2, pp. 194ff. and Ravaisse, "Essai," I, 425.

A Description of the City of Old Cairo

The city of Old Cairo is situated on a promontory. To the east of the city is a hill, not too high, of rock and stone. On one side of the city is the Ebn Tulun Mosque, built on a rise with two reinforced walls. With the exception of the walls of Āmed and Mayyāfāreqin, I never saw the likes of this mosque. It was built by one of the Abbasid emirs who was governor of Egypt. During the reign of al-Hākem be-Amr Allāh, the grandfather of the present sultan, the descendants of Ebn Tulun sold the mosque to al-Hākem for thirty thousand dinars. Later, they were about to have the minaret torn down when al-Hākem sent word to them to inquire what they were doing, since they had sold him the mosque. They replied that they had not sold the minaret, so he gave them another five thousand dinars for it. During the month of Ramadān the sultan prays there, and also on Fridays.

The city of Old Cairo was built on a hill for fear of the Nile waters. Once the site was just large boulders, but they have all been broken up and the ground leveled. Now they call such a place *ʿaqaba*. Looking at Old Cairo from a distance, because of the way it is situated, you would think it's a mountain. There are places where the houses are fourteen stories tall and others seven. I heard from a reliable source that one person has on top of a seven-story house a garden where he raised a calf. He also has a waterwheel up there turned by this ox to lift water from a well down below. He has orange trees and also bananas and other fruit-bearing trees, flowers, and herbs planted on the roof.

I was told by a credible merchant that there are many houses in Old Cairo where chambers can be hired. These chambers are thirty cubits square and can hold 350 people. There are also bazaars and lanes there where lamps always must be kept lit because no light ever falls upon the ground where people pass to and fro.

In Old Cairo alone, not counting New Cairo, there are seven cathedral mosques built one next to the other. In the two cities there are fifteen Friday mosques, so that on Fridays there is a sermon and congregation everywhere.

In the midst of the bazaar is the Bāb al-Jawāmeʿ Mosque, built by ʿAmr son of al-ʿĀṣ when he was appointed governor of Egypt by Moʿāwiya. The mosque is held aloft by four hundred marble columns, and the wall that contains the *mehrāb* is all slabs of white marble on which the entire Koran is written in beautiful script. Outside, on all four sides, are bazaars into which the mosque gates open. Inside there are always teachers and Koran- readers, and this mosque is the promenade of the city, as there are never less than five thousand people—students, the indigent, scribes who write checks and money drafts, and others. Al-Hākem bought this mosque from the descendants of ʿAmr son of al-ʿĀs. As they were in financial distress, they had asked the sultan to give permission for them to tear down the mosque their ancestor had built in order to sell the stones and bricks. Al-Hākem gave them one hundred thousand dinars for the mosque with all the people of Old Cairo as witnesses. Then he built many amazing things there, one of which is a silver lampholder with sixteen branches, each of which is 1½ cubits long. Its circumference is 24 cubits, and it holds seven hundred-odd lamps on holiday evenings. The weight is said to be 25 kantars of silver, a kantar being 100 rotls, a rotl being 144 silver dirhems. After it had been made, it was too large to get in through any of the existing doors, so they removed one of the doors and got it inside, after which the door was replaced. There are always ten layers of colored carpets spread one on top of the other in this mosque, and every night more than one hundred lamps are kept burning. The court of the chief justice is located here.

On the north side of the mosque is a bazaar called Suq al-Qanādil [Lamp Market], and no one ever saw such a bazaar anywhere else. Every sort of rare goods from all over the world can be had there: I saw tortoise-shell implements such as small boxes, combs, knife handles, and so on. I also saw extremely fine crystal, which the master craftsmen etch most beautifully. [This crystal] had been imported from the Maghreb, although they say that near the Red Sea, crystal even finer and more translucent than the Maghrebi variety had been found. I saw elephant tusks from Zanzibar, many of which weighed more than two hundred maunds. There was a type of skin from Abyssinia that resembled leopard, from which they make sandals. Also from Abyssinia was a domesticated bird, large with white spots and a crown like a peacock's.

Throughout Egypt is much honey and sugarcane. On the

third of the month of Day of the Persian year 416 I saw the following fruits and herbs, all in one day: red roses, lilies, narcissi, oranges, citrons, apples, jasmine, basil, quince, pomegranates, pears, melons, bananas, olives, myrobalan, fresh dates, grapes, sugarcane, eggplants, squash, turnips, radishes, cabbage, fresh beans, cucumbers, green onions, fresh garlic, carrots, and beets. No one would think that all of these fruits and vegetables could be had at one time, some usually growing in autumn, some in spring, some in summar, and some in fall. I myself have no ulterior motive in reporting all this, and I have recorded what I saw with my own eyes, although I am not responsible for some of the things I only heard, since Egypt is quite expansive and has all kinds of climate, from the tropical to the cold; and produce is brought to the city from everywhere and sold in the markets.

In Old Cairo they make all types of porcelain, so fine and translucent that one can see one's hand behind it when held up to the light. From this porcelain they make cups, bowls, plates, and so forth and paint them to resemble the *buqalamun* so that different colors show depending on how the article is held. They also produce a glass so pure and flawless that it resembles chrysolite, and it is sold by weight.

I heard from a reputable draper that they buy a stone-dirhem's weight of thread for 3 Maghrebi dinars, which is equal to 3½ Nishapuri dinars. In Nishapur I priced the very best thread available there and was told that one dirhem-weight of the finest was sold for 5 dirhems.

The city of Old Cairo is situated laterally along the Nile and has many kiosks and belvederes so that the people could draw water in buckets directly from the river; however, all water for the city is handled by water carriers, some by camel and some on their backs. I saw brass pitchers, each of which held three maunds of water, and one would think they were made of gold. I was told that there is a woman who leases out no less than five thousand of these pitchers for one dirhem a month each. When returned, the pitchers must be in perfect condition.

Opposite the city of Old Cairo is an island in the Nile that at one time was turned into a city. It is to the west of Old Cairo and has a Friday mosque and gardens. The island is a rock in the middle of the river, and I estimated each branch of the river to be the size of the Oxus, but the water flows gently and slowly.

Between the city and the island is a bridge made of thirty-six pontoons. Part of the city is on the other side of the river and is called Giza. There is also a Friday mosque there but no bridge, so you have to cross by ferry or canoe. There are more ships and boats in Old Cairo than in Baghdad and Basra combined.

The merchants of Old Cairo are honest in their dealings, and if one of them is caught cheating a customer, he is mounted on a camel with a bell in his hand and paraded about the city, ringing the bell and crying out, "I have committed a misdemeanor and am suffering reproach. Whosoever tells a lie is rewarded with public disgrace." The grocers, druggists, and peddlers furnish sacks for everything they sell, whether glass, pottery, or paper; therefore, there is no need for shoppers to take their own bags with them. Lamp oil is derived from turnip seed and radish seed and is called "*zayt hārr*." Sesame is scarce, and the oil derived from it is expensive, while olive oil is cheap. Pistachios are more expensive than almonds, and marzipan is not more than one dinar for ten maunds. Merchants and shopkeepers ride on saddled donkeys, both coming and going to and from the bazaar. Everywhere, at the heads of lanes, donkeys are kept saddled and ready, and anyone may ride them for a small fee. It is said that every day fifty thousand beasts are saddled for hire. No one other than soldiers and militiamen rides a horse, while merchants, peasants, and craftsmen ride donkeys. I saw many a dappled donkey, much like horses, but more delicate. The people of the city were extremely wealthy when I was there.

In the year 439 [A.D. 1047] the sultan ordered general rejoicing for the birth of a son: the city and bazaars were so arrayed that, were they to be described, some would not believe that drapers' and moneychangers' shops could be so decorated with gold, jewels, coins, goldspun cloth, and embroidery that there was no room to sit down!

The people are so secure under the sultan's reign that no one fears his agents, and they rely on him neither to inflict injustice nor to have designs on anyone's property. I saw such personal wealth there that were I to describe it, the people of Persia would never believe it. I could discover no end or limit to their wealth, and I never saw such ease and comfort anywhere.

I saw one man, a Christian and one of the most propertied men in all Egypt, who was said to possess untold ships, wealth, and property. In short, one year the Nile failed and the price of grain rose so high that the sultan's grand vizier summoned this Christian and said, "It has not been a good year. The sultan is burdened with the care of his subjects. How much grain can you give, either for sale or as a loan?" The Christian replied, "For the happiness of the sultan and the vizier, I have enough grain in readiness to guarantee Egypt's bread for six years." At that time there were easily five times the population of Nishapur in Cairo, so that anyone who knows how to estimate can figure out just how much grain he must have had. What a happy citizenry and a just ruler to have such conditions in their days! What wealth must there be for the ruler not to inflict injustice and for the peasantry not to hide anything!

I saw a caravanserai there called Dār al-Wazir where nothing but flax was sold, and on the lower floor there were tailors while above were specialists in clothing repair. I asked the keeper how much the fee for this caravanserai was. He told me that it was twenty thousand dinars per year but that just then one corner had been demolished for reconstruction so that only one thousand a month, or twelve thousand per year, was being collected. They said that there were two hundred caravanserais in the city the size of this one and even larger.

A Description of the Sultan's Banquet

It is customary for the sultan to give a banquet twice a year, on the two great holidays, and to hold court for both the elite and the common people, the elite in his presence and the commoners in other halls and places. Having heard a great deal about these banquets, I was very anxious to see one with my own eyes, so I told one of the sultan's clerks with whom I had struck up a friendship that I had seen the courts of the Persian sultans, such as Sultan Mahmud of Ghazna and his son Masʿud, who were great potentates enjoying much prosperity and luxury, and now I wanted to see the court of the Prince of the Faithful. He therefore spoke a word to the chamberlain, who was called the Sāheb al-Setr.

The last of Ramadān 440 [8 March 1049] the hall was decorated for the next day, which was the festival, when the sultan was to come after prayer and preside over the feast. Taken by my friend, as I entered the door to the hall, I saw constructions, galleries, and porticos that would take too long to describe adequately. There were twelve square structures, built one next to the other, each more dazzling than the last. Each measured one hundred cubits square, and one was a thing sixty cubits square with a dais placed the entire length of the building at a height of four ells, on three sides all of gold, with hunting and sporting scenes depicted thereon and also an inscription in marvelous calligraphy. All the carpets and pillows were of Byzantine brocade and *buqalamun*, each woven exactly to the measurements of its place. There was an indescribable latticework balustrade of gold along the sides. Behind the dais and next to the wall were silver steps. The dais itself was such that if this book were nothing from beginning to end but a description of it, words would still not suffice. They said that fifty thousand maunds of sugar were appropriated for this day for the sultan's feast. For decoration on the banquet table I saw a confection like an orange tree, every branch and leaf of which had been executed in sugar, and thousands of images and statuettes in sugar. The sultan's kitchen is outside the palace, and there are always fifty slaves attached to it. There is a subterranean passageway between the building and the kitchen, and the provisioning is such that every day fourteen camel-loads of ice are used in the royal sherbet-kitchen. Most of the emirs and the sultan's entourage received emoluments there, and, if the people of the city make requests on behalf of the suffering, they are given something. Whatever medication is needed in the city is given out from the harem, and there is also no problem in the distribution of other ointments, such as balsam.

The Conduct of the Sultan

The security and welfare of the people of Egypt have reached a point that the drapers, moneychangers, and jewelers do not even lock their shops—they only lower a net across the front, and no one tampers with anything.

There was once a Jewish jeweler who was close to the sultan and who was very rich, having been entrusted with buying all the sultan's jewels. One day soldiers rose up against this Jew and killed him. After this act was committed, and fearing the sultan's wrath, twenty thousand mounted horsemen appeared in the public square. When the army appeared thus in the field, the populace was in great fear. Until the middle of the day the horseman remained in the square, when finally a servant of the sultan came out of the palace, stood by the gate, and addressed them as follows: "The sultan asks whether you are in obeisance or not." They all cried out at once, saying, "We are his slaves and obedient, but we have committed a crime." "The sultan commands you to disperse immediately," said the servant, and they departed. The murdered Jew was named Abu Sa'id, and he had a son and a brother. They say that God only knows how much money he had. They also say that he had on the roof of his house three hundred silver pots with fruit trees planted in them so as to form a garden. The brother then wrote a note to the sultan to the effect that he was prepared to offer the treasury two hundred thousand dinars immediately for protection. The sultan sent the note outside to be torn up in public and said, "You rest secure and return to your home. No one will harm you, and we have no need of anyone's money." And they were compensated [for their loss].

From Syria to Qayrawān, which is as far as I went, in all towns and villages, mosque expenses, such as lamp oil, carpets, mats and rugs, salaries for custodians, janitors, muezzins, and so on, are handled by the sultan's agents. One year the governor of Syria wrote to ask if, since oil was scarce, if would be permissible to use *zayt hārr* in the mosque. In reply, he was told that he was to obey orders, that he was not a vizier, and that furthermore it was not licit to institute change in things pertaining to the House of God.

The chief justice receives a monthly stipend of two thousand dinars, and thus every judge down the scale so that the people need not fear venality from the bench.

It is customary for a representative of the sultan to appear in the mosques in the middle of the month of Rajab and proclaim the following: "O company of Muslims! The Pilgrimage season is at hand, and the sultan, as usual, has undertaken the outfitting of soldiers, horses and camels, and provisions." During Ramadān this proclamation is repeated, and from the first of Dhu'l-Qaʿda people set out for the appointed meeting place. At the middle of Dhu'l-Qaʿda the caravan moves out. The daily disbursement to the soldiers for fodder is one thousand dinars, over and above the twenty dinars each man receives per diem for the twenty-five days until they reach Mecca, where they stay for ten days. Thus, with the twenty-five days it takes them to return, they are gone for two months, and sixty thousand dinars are spent for provisions, not counting miscellaneous disbursements for rents, bonuses, stipends, and camels that die.

In the year 439 [A.D. 1048] an edict of the sultan to this effect was read to the people: "The Prince of the Faithful proclaims that in this year, owing to drought and the resulting scarcity of goods, which has caused the deaths of many, it is unwise for pilgrims to undertake the journey to the Hejaz. This we say in Muslim commiseration." Therefore, the pilgrims were held in abeyance until the next year, although the sultan did send the covering for the Kaʿba as usual, which he does twice a year. This very year, since the covering was being sent via the Red Sea, I went along.

On the first of Dhu'l-Qaʿda [18 April 1048] I left Egypt, and we reached the Red Sea on the 8th. From there we traveled for fifteen days by boat until we arrived at the town called al-Jār. It was the 22nd of the month. From there it is a four-day journey to Medina, which is a town on the edge of a salty, barren desert. It has running water, although not much, and is a palm grove. In that locale the *qebla* is directly south. The Prophet's Mosque is as large as the Harām Mosque in Mecca, and the grating around the Prophet's tomb is next to the pulpit. It is to the left when facing the *qebla*; and so, when the preacher mentions the Prophet from the pulpit, he turns to his right and points to the tomb. The tomb is pentagonal, and there are walls all around the five piers. Around the tomb is a balustrade so that no one can go in. There is also a net stretched across the top so that birds cannot enter. Between the tomb and the pulpit is a grating of marble that is called al-Rawda [The Garden], and it is said to be one of the gardens of Paradise, since the Prophet said, "Between my grave and my pulpit is one of the gardens of Paradise." The Shiʿites say that the tomb of Fātema Zahrā is there also. The mosque has a gate. Outside the city to the south is a plain and cemetery called Qobur al-Shohadā' [Tombs of the Martyrs], where Hamza son of ʿAbd al-Mottāleb is buried.

We stayed in Medina for two days; then, as time was short, we left. The road leads to the east. Two stations outside of Medina is a mountain and a defile called Johfa, which is the *miqāt* for Syria, the Maghreb, and Egypt (a *miqāt* being the place where the pilgrims put on the *ehram* [pilgrimage garb]). They say that one year many pilgrims had stopped there when suddenly a flash-flood swept down and killed them all, which is why it is called "Johfa" ["sweeping away"]. From Medina to Mecca is one hundred parasangs, but the whole way is easy and took us eight days.

On Sunday the 6th of Dhu'l-Hejja [23 May 1048] we arrived in Mecca and entered through the al-Safā Gate. As there had been a drought in Mecca that year, four maunds of bread cost one Nishapuri dinar. The *mojāwer*s were leaving the city, and no pilgrims had come from anywhere at all. On Wednesday, with the help of God, we completed the pilgrimage rites at ʿArafāt. Afterwards we stayed on in Mecca for only two days.

Because of hunger and misery people were fleeing the Hejaz in every direction. At this juncture I will not explain the Pilgrimage or describe Mecca. I will describe what I saw the next time I went to Mecca, when I remained as a *mojāwer* for six months.

When I returned to Egypt, it had been seventy-five days [from the time I left]. This year thirty-five thousand people came to Egypt from the Hejaz; and, since they were all hungry and naked, they received clothing and a pension from the sultan until the next year, when the rains came and food was once again plentiful enough in the Hejaz to support these people. The sultan gave them all clothing and gifts and sent them back home.

During Rajab 440 [January 1049] the sultan's representative announced once again that there was famine in the Hejaz and that, since it was unwise to go on the Pilgrimage, the people should excuse themselves from this obligation and adhere to God's commandment.[23] This year also no pilgrims went, although there was no shirking the sultan's duty, and therefore

[23]That is, the Koranic injunction of pilgrimage (3:97) is interpreted to mean that the Pilgrimage is *not* incumbent upon those who are unable to attend because of poverty, illness, or some other pressing cause (such as the famine spoken of here). Alternative rites to attendance at Mecca are given in Koran 2:196.

the covering for the the Kaʿba, servants, retinue for the emirs of Mecca and Medina, the gift for the emir of Mecca (the stipend for each being three thousand dinars a month), a horse, and a robe of honor, which are sent twice yearly, were duly expedited. This year a man called Qādi ʿAbd Allāh, a judge from Syria, was entrusted with these duties. I went in his company via Qolzom. This time the boat reached al-Jār on the 25th of Dhu'l-Qaʿda [1 May]. The season of the Pilgrimage being near, a camel could not be hired for less than five dinars. We traveled in haste and arrived in Mecca on the 8th of Dhu'l-Hejja [14 May]. With the help of God, we performed the Pilgrimage.

A large caravan from the Maghreb had come to Medina, and at the gates of Medina some Arabs had demanded protection money from them on the way back from the Pilgrimage. A fight broke out, leaving more than two thousand Maghrebis killed, and not many ever returned home. On this same Pilgrimage a group from Khorasan had come by land by way of Syria and Egypt and then by boat to Medina. On the 6th of Dhu'l-Hejja, as they still had 104 parasangs to go to ʿArafāt, they had said that they would give forty dinars each to anyone who could get them to Mecca within the three remaining days in order for them to perform the Pilgrimage. Some Arabs came forth and got them to ʿArafāt in two and a half days: they took their money, tied them each to a fast camel, and drove them from Medina. When they arrived at ʿArafāt, two of them had died still tied to the camels; the other four were more dead than alive. At the afternoon prayer as we were standing there, they arrived unable to stand up or to speak. They finally told us that they had pleaded with the Arabs to keep the money they had given but to release them, as they had no more strength to continue. The Arabs however, heedless of their entreaties, kept driving the camels forward. In the end the four of them made the Pilgrimage and returned via Syria.

Having performed the Pilgrimage, I returned to Egypt, since I had my books there and had no intention of returning.

The emir of Medina came that year to Egypt, since the sultan customarily gave him a yearly stipend because he was a descendant of Hosayn son of ʿAli. I was with him on the boat up to Qolzom. From there we continued in each other's company to Cairo.

In the year 441, while I was in Egypt, news arrived that the king of Aleppo, whose ancestors had been kings of Aleppo, had rebelled against the sultan his overlord. The sultan had a servant called ʿOmdat al-Dawla, who was the emir of the *matālebi*s and enormously rich and propertied. (*Matālebi* is what they call the people who dig for buried treasure in the graves of Egypt. From the Maghreb and the lands of Egypt and Syria come people who endure many hardships and spend a lot of money in those graves and rock piles. Many a time buried treasure is discovered, although often much outlay is made without anything being found. They say that in those places the wealth of the pharaohs is buried. Whenever anyone does find something, one-fifth is given to the sultan and the rest belongs to the finder.) At any rate, the sultan dispatched this ʿOmdat al-Dawla to that province with great pomp and circumstance, outfitting him with all the trappings of kings, such as canopies, pavilions, and so on. When he reached Aleppo he waged war and was killed. He had so much wealth that it took two months for it to be transferred from his treasury to the sultan's. He had three hundred slave-girls, most of them beauties, a few of whom were of the type taken to concubinage. The sultan ordered them to be given their choice of taking a husband or, if such was not their choice, having the remainder of the man's unencumbered estate so that they might remain in their own house, no command or force being exerted upon any of them. When the man was killed in Aleppo, the king was afraid the sultan would dispatch his army, so he sent the sultan his seven-year-old son along with his wife and many gifts and presents. He also offered apologies for his past conduct. When they arrived they were kept waiting outside the city for nearly two months. Neither were they admitted into the city nor were the presents accepted until finally, when all the judges of the city interceded on their behalf at court, they were admitted with honors.

Among other things, if any one wants to make a garden in Egypt it can be done during any season at all, since any tree, fruit-bearing or other, can be obtained and planted. There are special people, called *dallāl*s, who can obtain immediately any kind of fruit you desire, because they have trees planted in tubs on rooftops. Many roofs are gardens and most of what is grown is fruit-producing, such as oranges, pomegranates, apples, quince, roses, herbs, and vegetables. When a customer wishes, porters will go and tie the tubs to poles and carry the trees wherever desired. They will also make a hole in the ground and sink the tubs if wished. Then, when someone so desires, they will dig the tubs up and carry their fragments away, and the trees will not know the difference. I have never seen or heard of such a thing anywhere else in the world, and it is truly clever!

The Voyage to Mecca

Now I will describe my return voyage to Mecca from Egypt. I performed the prayer of the Feast [of Sacrifice] in Cairo and departed by boat on Tuesday, the 14th of Dhu'l-Hejja 441 [9 May 1050], bound for Upper Egypt, which is to the south and is the province through which the Nile flows before reaching Cairo. It is part of the realm of Egypt, and most of Egypt's prosperity derives from there. All along the banks of the Nile are too many towns and villages to describe. Finally, we reached a city called Asyut, an opium-producing region.

Opium is derived from a poppy with a black seed. When the seed grows and forms a pod, it is crushed and a molasses-like syrup comes out. This is collected and preserved, for it is opium. The poppy seed is small and like cumin.

In Asyut they weave turbans from sheep's wool unequaled anywhere in the world. The fine woolens imported into Persia and called "Egyptian" are all from Upper Egypt, since wool is not woven in Egypt proper. In Asyut I saw a shawl of sheep's wool the likes of which I saw neither in Lahore nor in Multan. It was so fine you would think it was silk.

From there we went on to a town called Akhmim, where I saw huge stone edifices that would amaze anyone who saw them. There is an ancient town with a stone wall. Most buildings there are made of twenty-thousand-maund and thirty-thousand-maund stones. What is really amazing is that there is no mountain or quarry within ten or fifteen parasangs of this place, so you wonder from where and how they were brought there.

Next we came to a town called Qus, which is a crowded and prosperous place. There are, in addition to a fortified wall, many date groves and orchards. We remained there for twenty days because there were two routes from here, one through arid desert and the other by river, and we could not decide which way to take. In the end we proceeded by river and reached Aswan. To the south of this city is a mountain, and the river Nile comes out of a defile in the mountain. It is said that boats can proceed no farther up the river because the water flows through narrow defiles and also because of large rocks coming down. Four parasangs from this city is the province of Nubia, the population of which is all Christian. The king of this province continually sends gifts to the sultan of Egypt and makes treaties so that Egyptian soldiers will not enter his land and molest the populace. The city of Aswan is very strong lest anyone attack from the direction of Nubia. There is a permanent garrison stationed there to defend the city and province. Opposite the city in the middle of the Nile is an island, which is like a garden, with date groves, olives, and other trees and crops irrigated by waterwheels. There I remained for twenty-one days because there was a large desert before us to cross and two hundred parasangs to the shore. It was the time for returning pilgrims to be arriving by camel. We were waiting until the camels were returned to hire one and then set off. While in Aswan I came to know a man called Abu ʿAbd Allāh Mohammad son of Falij. He was a pious and righteous man and knew something about logic. He helped me to inspect and hire a camel, which I got for one and a half dinars.

On the 5th of Rabiʿ I 442 [28 July 1050], having gone eight parasangs southeast, we came to a station called Dayqa, which is in a valley in the desert and surrounded on two sides by wall-like mountains. Between the two is an open space one hundred cubits wide where a well had been dug; the water was plentiful but not very good. Past this place there are five days of desert with no water whatsoever, so each person had to draw a jar of water. Next we came to a station called Hawd, which is a stone mountain with two holes from which water flows. The water stays in a pool and is fresh, but someone has to go inside one of the holes to bring out water for the camels. It had been seven days since the camels had been watered or fed, since there had been no [water or pasturage]. The camels stopped once every twenty-four hours, from the time the sun got hot in the day until the afternoon prayer, and they proceeded the rest of the day and night. The stopping-places are all known, because you cannot stop just anywhere, since there might not be anything to burn, and only in stopping-places can camel dung be found to burn for cooking. It was almost as though the camels themselves knew that if they poked along they would die of thirst; they did not need to be driven and, setting their own direction, went of their own accord, although there was no trace whatsoever of a road. Always headed east, there were stretches of fifteen parasangs with little water, only brackish, and stretches of thirty and forty parasangs with no water at all. On the 20th of Rabiʿ I 442 [12 August 1050] we reached the town of ʿAydhāb, having traveled from Aswan about two hundred parasangs in fifteen days.

The town of ʿAydhāb is situated by the sea and has a Friday mosque and a population of five hundred. It belongs to the sultan of Egypt and is a customs station for ships coming from Abyssinia, Zanzibar, and the Yemen. From there goods are transported by camel across the desert, the same way we had come, to Aswan and thence by boat to Cairo. To the right of this town, facing the *qebla*, is a mountain beyond which is a large desert with many herbivorous animals and people called the Bajāwis. This nation has no religion and has had no prophet or spiritual leader because they are so far from civilization. They inhabit a desert more than one thousand parasangs long and three hundred wide. In all this expanse there are not more than two small hamlets, one called Bahr al-Naʿām and the other ʿAydhāb. The desert runs lengthwise from Egypt to Abyssinia, which is from north to south, and across from the Nubian River to the Red Sea, from west to east. This nation, the Bajāwis, who live in this desert, are not a bad people and do not steal or make raids but tend their flocks. Muslims and others, however, kidnap their children and take them to sell in the cities of Islam.

The Red Sea is a gulf that splits off from the ocean at Aden and goes northward to the hamlet of Qolzom. Every place on the coast of this gulf where there is a town is called *bāz*, for example, there is a place in Qolzom, ʿAydhāb, and Bahr al-Naʿām that is so called. More than three hundred islands are said to be in the Red Sea, and ships bring oil and dried curds from there. There are said to be many cows and sheep on these islands, and the inhabitants are said to be Muslims, some belonging to Egypt and others to the Yemen.

In the hamlet of ʿAydhāb there is no water from wells or springs, only rainwater. When rain fails, the Bajāwis bring water to sell. During the three months we were there, we bought water at the rate of one or two dirhems a jug.

As the wind was northerly and we needed a southerly wind, the ship could not sail. When the people saw me, they asked me to preach to them. I obliged and acted as preacher until the winds changed and the boats could sail north and thence on to Jidda. They said that nowhere were such good camels to be had as in that desert, and they are exported even to Egypt and the Hejaz.

In the town of ʿAydhāb a man whose word I trust told me that once a ship set out from that town for the Hejaz carrying camels for the emir of Mecca. One of the camels died so it was thrown overboard. Immediately a fish swallowed it whole, except for one leg that stuck out of the fish's mouth. Then another fish came and swallowed whole the fish that had swallowed the camel. That fish is called *qarsh.* I saw in that town a fish skin that in Khorasan is called *safan.* We in Khorasan had thought it was a kind of lizard, but here I saw that it was a fish because it had fins like a fish.

While in Aswan I had a friend, as I have said before, named Abu ʿAbd Allāh Mohammad son of Falij. For my arrival in ʿAydhāb he had written a letter to an agent he had there to the effect that the agent should give me whatever I required and write him to that effect so that he could settle the account. As I had been in ʿAydhāb for three months, and everything I had was spent, of necessity I presented myself to that person with the letter. He acted very politely and said, "Oh yes, I am holding a great deal of his money. You may just sign for any amount you require." I was surprised at Mohammad Falij's generosity, that, with no prior dealings [with me], he should be so kind. Had I been a rogue and of a mind to do such a thing, I could have taken a great sum of money from him by means of that letter. Anyhow, I took one hundred maunds of flour, which was extremely valuable there, and gave him a chit in that amount. He then sent the paper I had signed to Aswan, and before I departed from ʿAydhāb, a reply came from Mohammad Falij that he should give me whatever I might require from his funds there, and, even if he should give me out of his own pocket, it would be made good, for the Prince of the Faithful ʿAli son of Abu Tāleb had commanded, "The believer does not hold back or take advantage." I have included this little vignette so that my readers may know that people can rely on others, that generosity exists everywhere, and that there have been and still are noble men.

A Description of the City of Jidda

Jidda is a large city and has a strong wall on the edge of the sea. The population is five thousand. The city is situated to the north of the sea, has good bazaars, and the *qebla* of the Friday mosque faces east. Outside the city there are no buildings except a mosque known as the Mosque of the Prophet of God. The city has two gates, one toward the east and Mecca and the other toward the west and the sea. Going south along the coast from Jidda, you reach the Yemen via the city of Saʿda, which is fifty parasangs away. To the north is the town of al-Jār, which is in the Hejaz. There are no trees or cultivation in Jidda, and all produce is brought from the outlying countryside. It is twelve parasangs to Mecca, and the emir of Jidda, a vassal to the emir of Mecca, is Tāj al-Maʿāli son of Abu'l-Fotuh, who is also the emir of Medina. I went to see the emir of Jidda, and he was generous enough to exempt me from the customs duties that would have applied to me. When I passed through the Muslim Gate, he wrote to Mecca saying that I was a scholar and nothing was to be taken from me.

I left Jidda on Friday at the time of the afternoon prayer. On Sunday, the last of Jomādā II, I arrived at the gate to the city of Mecca. There were many people from the Hejaz and the Yemen for the minor pilgrimage (*ʿomra*) on the first of Rajab, which is a great season, like the Ramadān feast and the Pilgrimage time. As they are nearby and the way is easy, they come three times a year.

A Description of the City of Mecca

The city of Mecca is situated low in the midst of mountains such that from whatever direction you approach, the city cannot be seen until you are there. The tallest mountain near Mecca is Abu Qobays, which is round like a dome, so that if you shoot an arrow from the foot of the mountain it reaches its top. Abu Qobays is to the east of the city, so that if you should be in the Harām Mosque in the month of Day you see the sun rise from behind the top of the mountain. On top of the mountain is a stone stele said to have been erected by Abraham. The city lies on a plain between the mountains and measures only two arrow-shots square. The Harām Mosque is in the middle of the plain, and the city lanes and bazaars are built all around it. Wherever there is an opening in the mountain a rampart wall has been made with a gate. The only trees in the city are at the western gate to the Harām Mosque, called Bāb Ebrāhīm [Abraham's Gate], where there are several tall trees around a well. On the eastern side of the Harām Mosque a large bazaar extends from south to north. At the south end is Abu Qobays. At the foot of Abu Qobays is Mount Safā', which is like a staircase, as rocks have been set in such a fashion that people can go up to pray, which is what is meant by [the expression] "to do Safā' and Marwa." At the other, the north end of the bazaar, is Mount Marwa, which is less tall and has many edifices built on it, as it lies in the midst of the city. In running between Safā' and Marwa the people run inside this bazaar.

For people who have come from faraway places to perform the minor pilgrimage, there are milestones and mosques set up half a parasang away from Mecca, where they bind their *ehrām*. "To bind the *ehrām*" means to take off all sewn garments and to wrap an *ezār*, or seamless garment, about the waist and another about the body. Then, in loud voice, you say, "*Labbayk, allāhomma, labbayk*,"[24] and approach Mecca. When anyone already inside Mecca wants to perform the minor pilgrimage, he goes out to one of the markets, binds his *ehrām*, says the Labbayk and comes back into Mecca with an intention to perform the minor

[24]The words of the *labbayk* mean approximately "[thy servant] has answered thy call, O God."

pilgrimage. Having come into the city, you enter the Harām Mosque, approach the Kaʿba, and circumambulate to the right, always keeping the Kaʿba to your left. Then you go to the corner containing the Black Stone, kiss it, and pass on. When the Stone is kissed once again in the same manner, one *tawf*, or circumambulation, has been completed. This continues for seven *tawfs*, three times quickly and four slowly. When the circumambulation is finished, you go to Maqām Ebrāhim [Station of Abraham] opposite the Kaʿba and stand behind the Station. There you perform two *rakʿat*s called the "circumambulation prayer." Afterwards you go to the Well of Zamzam, drink some water, or rub some on the face, and leave the Harām Mosque by the Safā' Gate. Just outside this gate are the steps up Mount Safā', and here you face the Kaʿba and say the prescribed prayer, which is well known. When the prayer has been said, you come down from Safā' and go from south to north through the bazaar to Marwa. Passing through the bazaar, you go past the gates to the Harām Mosque where the Prophet ran and commanded others to run also. The length is about fifty paces, and on either side are two minarets. When the people coming from Safā' reach the first two minarets, they break into a run until they pass the other two at the other end of the bazaar. Then they proceed slowly to Marwa. Upon reaching the end they go up Marwa and recite the prescribed prayer. Then they return through the bazaar and repeat the run until they have gone four times from Safā' to Marwa and three times from Marwa to Safā', making seven runs the length of the bazaar. Coming down from Marwa the last time, you find a bazaar with about twenty barber-shops facing each other. You have your head shaven and, with the minor pilgrimage completed, come out of the Sanctuary. The large bazaar on the east side is called Suq al-ʿAttārin [Druggists' Market]. It has nice buildings, and all the shopkeepers are druggists. In Mecca there are two baths paved with a green stone from which flints are made.

I reckoned that there were not more than two thousand citizens of Mecca, the rest, about five hundred, being foreigners and *mojāwer*s. Just at this time there was a famine, with sixteen maunds of wheat costing one dinar, for which reason a number of people had left.

Inside the city of Mecca are hospices for the natives of every region—Khorasan, Transoxiana, the Iraq, and so on. Most of them, however, had fallen into ruination. The Baghdad caliphs had built many beautiful structures, but when we arrived some had fallen to ruin and others had been expropriated. All the well water in Mecca is too brackish and bitter to drink, but there are many large pools and *masnaʿas*, costing up to ten thousand dinars each, that catch the rainwater from the hills. When we were there, however, they were empty. A certain prince of Aden, known as Pesar-e [son of] Shāddel, had brought water underground to Mecca at great personal expense. This water was used to irrigate crops at ʿArafāt and was limited to there, although conduits had been constructed and a little water reached Mecca, but not inside the city; therefore, a pool had been made to collect the water, and water carriers drew the water and brought it to the city to sell. Half a parasang out on the Borqa road is a well called Bir al-Zāhed [the Ascetic's Well]. A nice mosque is located there, and the water is good. The water carriers also bring water from that place for sale.

The climate of Mecca is extremely hot. I saw fresh cucumbers and eggplants and end of the month of Bahman. This was the fourth time I had been to Mecca.

For the first of Rajab 442 [19 November 1050] until the 20th of Dhu'l-Hejja [5 May 1051] I was a *mojāwer* in Mecca. On the 15th of Farvardin the grapes were ripe and were brought to town from the villages to be sold in the market. On the first of Ordibehesht melons were plentiful. All kinds of fruit are available in winter, and [the markets] are never empty.

A Description of Arabia and the Yemen

One station south of Mecca is the province of the Yemen, which stretches along the coast. The Yemen and the Hejaz are contiguous, and both are Arabic-speaking. In local parlance the Yemen is called Hemyar and the Hejaz, Arabia. This land is bounded on three sides by water and is a peninsula. To the east is the Sea of Basra (Persian Gulf), to the west the Red Sea, which, as has already been mentioned, is a gulf, and to the south is the (Arabian) Ocean. The length of the peninsula that is the

Yemen and the Hejaz, from Kufa in the north to Aden in the south, is approximately five hundred parasangs. From Oman in the east to al-Jār in the west, the width is four hundred parasangs. Arabia extends from Kufa to Mecca, and Hemyar from Mecca to Aden. There is little civilization in Arabia, its people being desert nomads, herdsmen, and tent-dwellers.

Hemyar is divided into three sections. The first is Tehāma, which is bounded on the west by the Red Sea and has many towns and cities, such as Sa'da, Zabid, San'a, and others. These towns are on the plain. The king of this area is an Ethiopian vassal to Pesar-e Shāddel. The second section of Hemyar is a mountainous region called Najd, which has uncultivated regions and is cold, with narrow passes and strong fortresses. The third section lies to the east and contains many cities such as Najrān, 'Athr, Bisha, and others. This section is divided into many areas, each of which has a king or chieftain. There is no absolute potentate or ruler there. The people are rebellious, and most of them are thieves, murderers, and bandits. This area is 200 by 250 parasangs and contains many people of all sorts.

Ghomdān Castle is in the Yemen, in a city called San'a. Now, however, nothing much remains of the castle but a mound in the middle of the city. They say the lord of this castle used to rule the whole world and that there is much treasure buried in this mound; but no one, neither sultan nor peasant, has ever discovered anything. In the city of San'a they do work in agate, which is a stone mined in the mountains, then heated in sand over a stove and cured in sand in the sun. It is then ground against stone. In Egypt I saw a sword sent to the sultan from the Yemen that had a handle and pommel made of one solid piece of red agate; it looked like ruby!

A Description of the Harām Mosque and the Ka'ba

As I have already stated, the Ka'ba is situated in the middle of the Harām Mosque, which is in the middle of the city of Mecca. It runs lengthwise from east to west, and the breadth is on a north-south axis. The walls, however, do not meet at right angles, for the corners are rounded so that the whole is an oval shape, because when the people pray in this mosque they must face the Kaʿba from all directions. Where the mosque is longest, that is, from Abraham's Gate to the Bani Hāshem Gate, it measures 424 cubits. The width, from Bāb al-Nadwa [Council Gate] on the north to the Safā' Gate on the south, the widest point, is 304 cubits. Because of its oval shape, it is narrower in places and wider in others. Around the mosque are three vaulted colonnades with marble columns. In the middle of the structure a square area has been made. The long side of the vaulting, which faces the mosque courtyard, has forty-five arches, with twenty-three arches across the breadth. The marble columns number 184 in all and are said to have been ordered by the Baghdad caliphs and to have been brought by sea from Syria. The story goes that when these columns arrived in Mecca, the ropes that had been used to secure the columns on board ship and onto carts were cut and sold for sixty thousand dinars. One of the columns, a shaft of red marble, stands at the spot called al-Nadwa Gate; it is said to have been bought for its weight in dinars and is estimated at three thousand maunds.

There are eighteen doors in the Harām Mosque, all built with arches supported by marble columns, but none is set with a door that can be closed.[25] On the eastern side are four doors. Set in

[25]This passage presents a good deal of difficulty on the names of the gates around the sanctuary. Nāṣer says that the east wall has four gates (he names three), the south wall seven gates (he names six), the west wall three (he gives two), and the north wall four (he names five). Since the gates have changed their names over the centuries with the various repairs made to the sanctuary walls, as well as with topographical changes outside the sanctuary (not to mention the corrupt state of the *Safarnāma* text itself), it is almost impossible to say for certain which of Nāṣer's gates correspond to which gates as they were known earlier and/or later. A tentative correlation is given as follows:

On the *east wall*, (1) the first gate named by Nāṣer is the Bāb al-Nabi [The Prophet's Gate], also known as Bāb al-Janā'ez [Funeral Gate]. (2) The next gate on this wall is known as Bāb al-ʿAbbās [ʿAbbās's Gate] but is not named by Nāṣer. (3) The next gate is Bāb ʿAli [ʿAli's Gate], also known as Bāb Bani Hāshem [The Bani Hāshem Gate], in conformity with Nāṣer's report. I do not know what to make of Nāṣer's second gate at the southeastern corner, which, as he says, is also known as Bāb al-Nabi: he may mean Bāb al-ʿAbbās, which was known, along with Bāb al-Nabi, as Bāb al-Janā'ez. (4) The fourth gate on this wall, at the northeastern corner, would be the Bāb Bani Shayba [The Bani Shayba Gate], which Nāṣer lists with the gates of the north wall at the end of his report.

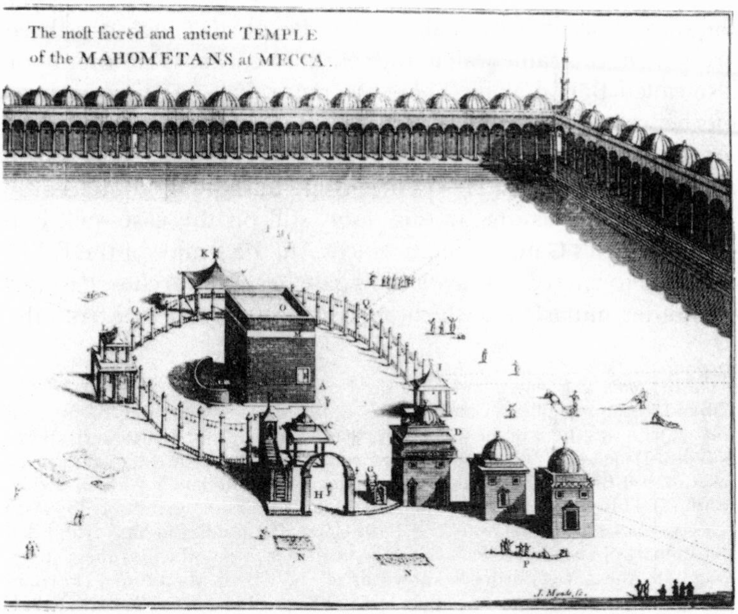
The most sacred and antient TEMPLE
of the MAHOMETANS at MECCA.

An engraving included in the 1731 edition of Joseph Pitts, *A True and Faithful Account of the Religion and Manners of the Mahometans.*

Legend (note that the engraving has been reversed):

A. The black stone, which the Arabians, long before Mahomet's time, had in great veneration. When the Carmathians after the taking of Mecca carried off this stone, they refused 5 thousand deniers [dinars] which were offered for restoring it. But after 22 years it was again reposited in its former place in the Caba [Ka'ba].

B. The white stone thought to have been Ishmael's Sepulchre; which is called by others the green pavement [Hejr].

C. Abraham's place [Maqām Ebrāhim] where they pretend to shew the marks of his feet.

D. The building in which is the well Zemzem [Zamzam], whose water is accounted salutary both to the Souls & bodies of those who drink it. [In Nāser's description the well had a much smaller covering.]

E. The gate of the Caba, consisting of two folding doors; to kiss this they ascend the stairs at G. & so are conveyed thither.

F. The pulpit in which they make harangues to the people.

G. The rolling stairs by which they ascend to the gate of the Caba.

H. The old gate.

I. The place for the Hanbelitae [Halbalites], one of the four chief Sects among the Mahometans.

K. The place of the Malekitae [Malikites], who are another of the Sects.

L. The place of the Hanifaei [Hanafites]. The Schafaei [Schafi'ites], meet in the place called Abraham's.

M. The golden fascia [*keswa*] fastened to a black silk veil of Damask, by which the external parts of the Caba are so closely covered, as no part of the walls is to be seen.

N. Pieces of tapestry spread on the floor to perform their devotions on.

O. The canal through which the water floweth from the top of the Caba on the stone called Ishmael's Sepulchre.

P. The place where vessels filled with the water of the well Zemzem are given to travellers to carry home with them.

Q. The inner boundary next the Caba which is illuminated in the night time with lamps [*mashā'*el].

[The two buildings above P., known as the Qobbatayn, "the two domes," are located approximately where Nāser describes the Seqāyat al- Hājj and Khezānat al- Zayt. Pitts was in Mecca in 1680.]

the north corner is the Bāb al-Nabi [Prophet's Gate] with three arches. On this same wall in the southern corner is another door also called Bāb al-Nabi. There are more than one hundred cubits between these two doors, and the latter has two arches. Exiting by this door, one is in the Druggist's Market, where the Prophet's house was. He used to come into the mosque to pray by this door. Passing by this door, still on the east wall, one comes to ʿAli's Gate, through which ʿAli, the Prince of the Faithful, used to enter for prayer. This gate has three arches. Past this is another minaret, to which one runs during the *saʿy* from the

On the *south wall* Nāṣer states that there are seven gates: (1) the gate he calls Bāb al-Daqqāqin [Fullers' Gate] should be the gate known as Bāb Bāzān. Ebn Jobayr, who was there in the 1180s, says that two of the south gates were known as Bāb al-Daqqāqin. (2) Nāṣer's "Bāb al-Fassānin" (?) should be the gate normally called Bāb al-Baghla [The Mule Gate], originally the Bāb Bani Sofyān b. ʿAbd al-Asad. (3) This is Bāb al-Ṣafā' [The Ṣafā' Gate], as all are agreed. (4–6) Nāṣer gives two names, Bāb al-Ṭowā [The Ṭowā Gate, after a valley in Mecca] and Bāb al-Tammārin [The Dateseller's Gate]: it is difficult to say which of these corresponds to the gates normally known as (4) Bāb Bani Makhzum [The Bani Makhzum Gate], also known as Bāb Ajyād al-Ṣaghir [The Small Ajyād Gate, after a hill in Mecca called Ajyād and Jayād], (5) Bāb al-Mojāhediyya, also known as Bāb al-Raḥma [The Mercy Gate] and Bāb Ajyād, and (6) Bāb Bani Taym [The Bani Taym Gate], later known as Bāb Madrasat al-Sharif ʿAjlān. (7) Nāṣer's "Bāb al-Maʿāmel" [Workshop Gate], outside of which was located Abu Jahl's house, is the Bāb Omm Hāni, also known as Bāb Abi Jahl and Bāb Ajyād al-Kabir [The Great Ajyād Gate].

On the *west wall*, Nāṣer says that there are three gates; however, he gives only two names: (1) his "Bāb ʿOrwa" is certainly a textual corruption of Bāb al-Ḥazwara, named for a marketplace that was incorporated into the sanctuary, and Bāb al-Wedāʿ [The Farewell Gate]. (2) His Bāb Ebrāhim [Abraham's Gate] is in conformity with other sources and is also known as Bāb al-Khayyāṭin [Tailors' Gate]. (3) This is unnamed by Nāṣer but must be the Bāb Bani Sahm, also known as Bāb al-ʿOmra [Minor Pilgrimage Gate] and Bāb Bani Jomaḥ.

On the *north wall*, according to Nāṣer, are four gates: (1) his Bāb al-Wasiṭ should be the gate known as Bāb al-Sodda and Bāb al-ʿAtiq [Ancient Gate]. (2) This is Bāb al-ʿAjala, as all sources are agreed, later known as Bāb al-Bāseṭiyya after the *madrasa* of ʿAbd al-Bāseṭ. (3) Bāb al-Nadwa [Council Gate] is also known as Bāb al-Ziyāda [Projection Gate]. Nāṣer does not mention the small gate into the Ziyāda known as Bāb al-Qoṭbi [Qoṭbi's Gate]. (4) Nāṣer's "Bāb al-Moshāwara" [Advisement Gate] must be the single gate usually known as Bāb al-Dorayba [Little Lane Gate]. The last gate named by Nāṣer, the Bāb Bani Shayba, has been reckoned in the east wall, above. See Abu'l-Walid Moḥammad b. ʿAbd Allāh al-Azraqi, *Akhbār Makka*, ed. Roshdi al-Ṣāleḥ Malḥas (Mecca: Dār al-Thaqāfa, 1385/1965), vol. 2, pp. 87ff.; Abu'l-Ḥosayn Moḥammad b. Jobayr, *Reḥlat Ebn Jobayr* (Beirut: Dār Ṣāder, 1384/1964), p. 82f.; Qoṭb al-Din Moḥammad Nahrwāli, *al-Eʿlām be-aʿlām bayt allāh al-harām* (Mecca: ʿElmiyya, 1370/1950), pp. 348ff.; R. F. Burton, *Personal Narrative of a Pilgrimage to al-Madinah & Meccah* (New York: Dover, 1964), vol. 2, p. 314.

Bani Hāshem Gate, and which is one of the four minarets previously described.

In the south wall, which forms the length of the mosque, are seven gates. The first, at the corner and semicircular in shape, is Bāb al-Daqqāqin [Fullers' Gate] and has two arches. Slightly to the west is another two-arched gate called Bāb al-Fassānin [?]. At an equal distance is the al-Safā' Gate which has five arches. This middle gate is the largest of all and has two small arches on either side. It was by this gate that the Apostle of God went out to Safā' to pray. The threshold of this middle gate is of a large white stone, although it once was black. The Apostle placed his holy foot there and left an imprint. This footprint was later cut out of the black stone and set into the white stone so that the toes face inside the mosque. For a blessing, some pilgrims place their foreheads on this print and others, their feet. I thought it more fitting to place my head thereupon. A bit to the west of the al-Safā' Gate is the Bāb al-Towā, which has two arches. A little farther on is the Bāb al-Tammārin, again with two arches. Past this is the Bāb al-Maʿāmel, with two arches. Directly facing this gate is Abu Jahl's house, which is now used as a privy.

In the western wall, the width of the mosque, there are three gates, the first of which is in the south corner and is called Bāb ʿOrwa. It has two arches. In the middle of this side is the Abraham's Gate, which has three arches.

In the north or long wall there are four gates: in the west corner is Bāb al-Wasit with one arch; to the east is the Bāb al-ʿAjala with one arch; in the middle of the side is the Bāb al-Nadwa with two arches; past that is the Bāb al-Moshāwara with one arch, and finally at the northeast corner is the Bāb Bani-Shayba.

The Kaʿba stands in the middle of the courtyard and is rectangular, with the length on a north–south axis. It is seventeen cubits long, thirty [high], and sixteen wide. The door is toward the east. Entering the Kaʿba, you find the Iraqi corner on the right, the Black Stone corner on the left, the Yemen corner at the southwest, and the Syrian corner at the northwest. The Black Stone is set in a large stone in one corner of the Kaʿba at about the height of a man's chest.

The Shape of the Stone

The Black Stone is oval in shape, one hand, four fingers long and eight fingers wide. From the Black Stone to the door of the Kaʿba is four cubits. The space between the Stone and the Kaʿba door is called the Moltazem.[26] The door is four cubits off the ground so that when standing on tiptoe you can reach the threshold, although a wooden staircase wide enough for ten men abreast has been constructed so that you can get inside when necessary. The floor is raised as high as the door.

A Description of the Kaʿba Door

The door to the Kaʿba is made of teak and is a double door 6½ cubits tall. Each half is 1¾ ells wide so that the whole door is 3½ ells wide. The face of the door contains inscriptions and silver circles. The inscriptions are done in gold burnished with silver and contain the following Koranic verse: "Verily the first house appointed unto men to worship in was that which was in Becca."[27] Two large silver rings sent from Ghazna are attached to the door too high for anyone to reach. Two other silver rings, smaller than the first two, are attached to the doors such that anyone could reach them. To these lower rings is fitted a large silver lock, and the doors cannot be opened without removing it.

A Description of the Interior of the Kaʿba

The walls are six spans thick, and the floor is paved with white marble. Inside the structure are three small cabinets like platforms, one opposite the door, and the other two on the north

[26]al-Moltazem is the name given, as Nāṣer says, to the area of the Kaʿba wall between the Black Stone and the door into the interior. According to al-Azraqi it measures four cubits and is considered a particularly appropriate place to render special votive prayers, in continuation of pre-Islamic custom. See Yāqut, IV, 629.

[27]Koran 3:96. "Becca" is a variant of "Mecca".

side. The interior columns, which are attached to the ceiling, are made of teak wood and, except for one round one, are carved on all four sides. On the north side is a long, red marble slab set into the floor. It is said that the Apostle prayed on this slab, hence anyone who knows this tries to pray there also. The walls are faced with multicolored marble. On the western side are six silver *mehrāb*s nailed to the wall. Each one is a man's height and elaborately worked in gold and burnished in silver. These niches are raised off the floor. From the floor to a height of four cubits the walls are plain; above that height they are covered with marble up to the ceiling, elaborately decorated and mostly plated with gold. The tops to the three cabinets already mentioned, one each in the Iraq, Syria, and Yemen corners, are two wooden planks nailed to the walls with silver nails. These planks are from Noah's ark. Each one is five yards long and one yard wide. The top of the cabinet behind the Black Stone is draped with red brocade.

Inside the door, in the corner to the right, is a square structure three yards by three, in which there is a small door leading to the roof. A silver door is placed there and is called the Bāb al-Rahma [Gate of Mercy], and there is a silver lock affixed to the door. On the roof is another door, like a trap door, both sides of which are plated in silver. The ceiling is wooden, but it is all covered with brocade so that no wood is visible. Over the front wall is an inscription in gold with the name of the sultan of Egypt who took Mecca from the caliphs of the house of ʿAbbās, al-Moʿezz le-Din Allāh. There are four other large silver plaques nailed to the wall with silver nails, on each of which is the name of a sultan of Egypt who sent a plaque during his reign. Between the columns are hung three silver lamps. The roof of the Kaʿba is covered with Yemenite marble and looks like crystal. There are four skylights in the corners, and over each of these is a piece of glass, so that the light can come in but not the rain. The rain-spout is in the middle of the north side; it is three yards long and is covered with gold writing.

The covering of the Kaʿba is white and has embroidery in two places. The embroidery bands are one ell wide and are separated by a distance of about ten ells. The spaces above and below the embroidery are equal, so that by means of the bands, the height is divided into three segments ten ells each. On four sides of the covering are woven colored medallions geometrically decorated with gold thread. On each side are three medallions, a large one in the middle and a smaller one on either side. Thus the four sides contain a total of twelve medallions. On the north side, outside the building, is constructed a wall, about one and one-half ells high. Each end of this wall curves in toward a corner of the Kaʿba so that the wall is bowed and semicircular. The midpoint of this wall is fifteen yards away from the Kaʿba wall. The wall and ground of this place are paved in colored marble in designs. This place is called Hejr, and the water from the rainspout pours into this Hejr.[28] Beneath the rainspout is placed a green stone slab in the shape of a medallion, into which the water falls from the spout. The stone is large enough for a man to pray on.

Abraham's Station is to the east of the Kaʿba. It is a rock that has two imprints of Abraham's feet. It is placed in another stone and covered on all four sides up to a man's height by wood worked as finely as can be imagined, with silver drums affixed. On two sides the covering is bound with chains to the large rocks and with two locks so that no one can tamper with it. Between the Station and the Ka'ba is a space of thirty cubits.

The Well of Zamzam is forty-six cubits east of the Black Stone corner of the Kaʿba. The top of the well is 3½ ells square, and the water is brackish but can be drunk. The enclosure over the top is made of slabs of white marble two cubits tall, and all around the well are basins so that water may be poured for ablutions. The ground is covered with a latticed wooden grill beneath which the water flows away. The door to the structure is toward the east.

Opposite the Well of Zamzam, also to the east, is another square edifice with a dome. It is called Seqāyat al-Hājj [Pilgrims' Drinking Place] and holds water vats from which pilgrims drink.

To the east of the Seqāyat al-Hājj is another, rectangular

[28]The Ḥejr is the area between the north wall of the Kaʿba and the semicircular wall known as al-Ḥaṭim. The Ḥejr area contains the tombs of Ishmael and his mother Hagar and is supposed to have been part of the original Kaʿba of Abraham. When the Qoraysh rebuilt the Kaʿba ca. 595, the Ḥejr was left uncovered for lack of funds. The area was included in the rebuilding of ʿAbd Allāh b. Zobayr in 64/683 but was subsequently returned to the form in which the Qoraysh had left it by order of the caliph ʿAbd al-Malek in 74/693. See Yāqūt, II, 208; Burton, *Personal Narrative*, II, 306 and 322ff.

structure with three domes. It is called Khezānat al-Zayt [Oil Storage]; and candles, oil, and lamps are kept there.

All around the Ka'ba are columns, each pair of which are spanned with wooden beams carved in decorative designs. These beams have rings and hooks for suspending lamps and candleholders at night, and they are called *mashā'el.* Between the Ka'ba and the *mashā'el* is a space 150 ells across, which is where the circumambulation is performed.

The buildings in the courtyard of the Harām Mosque, not counting the magnificent Ka'ba, are three: the well of Zamzam, the Seqāyat al-Hājj, and the Khezānat al-Zayt.

Beneath the arcade next to the mosque wall are chests, one for each of the principal cities of the Maghreb, Egypt, Syria, Anatolia, the two Iraqs,[29] Khorasan, Transoxiana, and so on.

Four parasangs to the north of Mecca is a place called Borqa with running water and trees and two parasangs square in area, where the emir of Mecca and his army stay.

This year I remained as a *mojāwer* in Mecca from the first of Rajab. During that month it is customary to open the door to the Ka'ba every day at sunup.

A Description of the Opening of the Ka'ba Door

An Arab clan called the Banu Shayba holds the key to the Ka'ba. They function as servants to the House and receive a stipend and robes of honor from the sultan of Egypt. Their chief keeps possession of the key, and when he comes to the mosque, five or six persons accompany him. As they approach the building, ten or so pilgrims bring the stairs we have previously mentioned and place them at the door. The old man mounts and stands at the threshold, and to open the door, a man on either side of him holds back the brocade covering as though holding a great robe with which he has been vested. He opens the lock and removes it from the rings. A great number of pilgrims will have assembled at the door, and when it is opened, they raise their

[29]The "two Iraqs" are "Persian Iraq," or western Iran north of Khuzestān and south of Azerbaijan (also called Jebāl), and "Arab Iraq," or lower Mesopotamia.

hands and shout in prayer. Since the voices of the pilgrims can be heard throughout Mecca, all know that the Kaʿba door has been opened and, all at once, shout in prayer so that a great tumult fills the city. Then the old man goes inside, with the other two men holding back the covering, and prays two *rakʿats*. Both wings of the door are then opened and the chief, standing at the threshold, delivers a sermon in a loud voice and invokes blessings upon the Messenger of God and his family. Then the old man and his two assistants stand aside from the door, and the pilgrims begin to pour in. Everyone prays two *rakʿats* and then leaves. This continues until nearly noon. When praying inside the Kaʿba, you turn your face toward the door, although any other direction is also licit. I counted the number of people inside when the building was filled to capacity and reckoned 720.

The common people of the Yemen who come on the Pilgrimage look generally like Hindus: they wear lungis, have long hair and plaited beards, and carry Qatifi daggers called *kattāra* at their waists, like Hindus. They say that the Hindus originated from the Yemen, and that *kattāra* is originally from the Arabic *qattāla*.[30]

During the months of Shaʿbān, Ramadān, and Shawwāl, the door the the Kaʿba is opened on Mondays, Thursdays, and Fridays. When Dhu'l-Qaʿda comes, it is not opened again.

The Minor Pilgrimage from Jeʿrāna

Four parasangs north of Mecca is a place called Jeʿrāna, where Mohammad was with his army. On the 16th of Dhu'l-Qaʿda, he donned the *ehrām* and came from there to Mecca to make a minor pilgrimage. There are two wells there, one called Bir al-Rasul [the Well of the Apostle] and the other Bir ʿAli ebn Abi-Tāleb [ʿAli's Well]. The water of both is extremely good. They are ten yards apart. The custom [of the Prophet] is still maintained, and at the same time people make a minor pilgrimage. Nearby is a small hill with bowl-like depressions in the rock. It is

[30]The Indian double-pronged dagger is called *kaṭār* in Hindi (from the Sanskrit *kaṭṭārāh*) and is a loanword in Persian as *kattāra*. Nāṣer erroneously speculates that the word is derived from the Arabic *qattāla* ("killer").

said that the Prophet kneaded dough with his own hands in those depressions. For this reason people go there and knead dough with water from those wells. Kindling is gathered from the many trees about, and bread is baked to be taken back home as a blessing. In that same area is a high hill where Belāl the Abyssinian is said to have called out for prayer; hence people still go there to give the call to prayer. When I went, there was an enormous crowd, with more than a thousand camel litters stretching clear to the next well.

The route I took this time from Egypt to Mecca was three hundred parasangs. From Mecca to the Yemen is twelve parasangs.

The Plain of ʿArafāt lies in the midst of small, hump-backed mountains and is two parasangs square. There was once a mosque there built by Abraham, but now only a ruined brick pulpit remains. At the midday prayer, the preacher mounts this pulpit and delivers the sermon. Then the call to prayer is given and two *rakʿats* are accomplished in congregation, after the custom of travelers. After this, a prayer is made standing, and two more congregational prayers are done. Afterwards, the preacher mounts a camel and [everyone] goes off toward the east.

One parasang from there is a small stone mountain called Jabal al-Rahma [the Mount of Mercy], and here people stand and pray until the sun sets. Pesar-e Shāddel, who was the emir of Aden, had water brought some distance and at great expense from this mountain to the Plain of ʿArafāt, where he had cisterns constructed that are filled during the Pilgrimage season. This same Shāddel built a dome with four large arches on top of the Mount of Mercy so that during the day and night when people are at ʿArafāt, lamps visible for two parasangs can be lit atop the dome. It is said that the emir of Mecca took one thousand dinars before giving permission to build this structure.

On the 9th of Dhu'l-Hejja 442 [24 April 1051], with God's help, I completed my fourth Pilgrimage. After the sun had set and the pilgrims and preacher had left ʿArafāt, everyone traveled one parasang to Mashʿar al-Harām [Sacred Shrine], which is called Mozdalefa. Here a nice structure like a *maqsura* has been built for people to pray in. The stones that are cast in Mina are gathered up here. It is customary to spend the holiday eve in this spot and then to proceed to Mina early the next morning after the dawn prayer for making the sacrifice. A large mosque called Khayf is there, although it is not customary to deliver the sermon or to perform the holiday prayer at Mina, as the Prophet did not establish a precedent.

The tenth day is spent at Mina, and stones are cast, which practice is explained as a supererogatory act connected with the Pilgrimage.

On the twelfth, everyone who intends to leave departs directly from Mina, and those who intend to remain a while in Mecca go there. Hiring a camel from an Arab for the thirteen-day journey to Lahsā, I bade farewell to God's House.

On Friday the 19th of Dhu'l-Hejja 442 [4 May 1051], the first of the old month of Khordād, I traveled seven parasangs from Mecca. There was an open plain with a mountain visible in the distance. Heading toward that mountain, we passed by fields and villages. There was a well called Bir al-Hosayn ebn Salāma [the Well of Hosayn son of Salāma]. The weather was cold. We continued eastward, and on Monday the 22nd of Dhu'l-Hejja [7 May] arrived in Tā'ef, which is twelve parasangs from Mecca.

A Description of Tā'ef

Tā'ef is situated on top of a mountain, and in the month of Khordād it was so cold that you had to sit in the sun, whereas in Mecca melons had been plentiful. The entire district of Tā'ef consists of a wretched little town with a strong fortress. It has a small bazaar and a pitiful little mosque. There is running water, and pomegranate and fig trees abound. The tomb of ʿAbd Allāh son of ʿAbbās is there near the town. On this spot the Baghdad caliphs had constructed a large mosque which had incorporated the tomb into one corner, to the right of the *mehrāb* and pulpit. Now, however, people have built houses and live there. We left Tā'ef.

All along the way were mountains and rubble, and there were small fortresses and villages everywhere. In the midst of some rubble, they showed me a small, ruined fortress, which the

Arabs said had been Laylā's house, although they tell many such strange tales.[31] Further on, we came to a fortress called Motar, which is twelve parasangs from Tā'ef. From there, we proceeded to a district called Thorayyā, where there were many date-palm groves in which agriculture was maintained by means of irrigation from wells with waterwheels. There is said to be no ruler or sultan in that area: each place has an independent chieftain or headman. The people are robbers and murderers and constantly fight among themselves. This place is twenty-five parasangs from Tā'ef.

We continued on past that place and saw a fortress called Jazʿ. Within half a parasang we passed four fortresses, the largest of which, where we stopped, was called the Bani-Nosayr Fortress, and it had a few date palms.

As the man from whom I had hired my camel was from Jazʿ, I stayed there for fifteen days, there being no *khafir* [safe-conduct] to take us on farther. The Arab tribes of that region each have a particular territory in which they graze their flocks, and no stranger can enter one of these territories, since anyone who does not have a *khafir* will be captured and plundered. Therefore, from each tribe there is a *khafir*, who can pass through a given territory. The *khafir* is also called *qalāvoz.*

By chance, the leader of the Arabs with whom we had traveled, the Banu Sawād, came to Jazʿ, and we took him as our *khafir*. His name was Abu Ghānem ʿAbs son of al-Baʿir, and we set out under his protection. A group of Arabs, thinking they had found "prey" (as they call all strangers), came headed toward us; but since their leader was with us, they passed without saying anything. Had he not been with us, they most certainly would have destroyed us.

We had to remain among these people for a while because there was no *khafir* to take us further. Finally, we found two men to act as *khafirs* and paid them ten dinars each to take us to the next tribe.

Among one tribe, some seventy-year-old men told me that in their whole lives they had drunk nothing but camels' milk, since

[31] Laylā was the beloved of Qays, who, forbidden to marry her, roamed like a madman among the animals of the desert; hence he was called "Majnun" ("mad"). This story was well known among the Arabs and has also inspired several famous Persian romances on the subject.

in the desert there is nothing but bitter scrub eaten by the camels. They actually imagined that the whole world was like this!

Thus I was taken and handed over from tribe to tribe, the entire time in constant mortal danger. God, however, willed that we come out of there alive.

In the midst of an expanse of rubble, we reached a place called Sarbā, where there were mountains shaped like domes. I have never seen anything like them anywhere. They were not so high that an arrow could not have been shot to the top, and they were as bald and smooth as an egg, not the slightest crack or flaw showing.

Along the way, whenever my companions saw a lizard they killed and ate it. The Arabs, wherever they are, milk their camels for drink. I could neither eat the lizard nor drink camels' milk; therefore, wherever I saw a kind of bush that yielded small berries the size of a pea, I picked a few and subsisted on that.

Falaj

After enduring much hardship and suffering great discomfort, on the 23rd of Safar [6 July] we came to Falaj, a distance of 180 parasangs from Mecca. Falaj lies in the middle of the desert and had once been an important region, but internal strife had destroyed it. The only part left inhabited when we arrived was a strip half a parasang long and a mile wide. Inside this area there were fourteen fortresses inhabited by a bunch of filthy, ignorant bandits. These fourteen fortresses had been divided up between two rival factions who were constantly engaged in hostilities. They claimed to be the "Lords of al-Raqim" mentioned in the Koran.[32] They had four irrigation canals for their palm grove, and their fields were on higher ground and watered from wells. They plow with camels, not cows. As a matter of fact, I never saw a cow there. They produce very little in the way of agriculture, and each man has to ration himself with two seers of grain a day. This is baked as bread and suffices from the evening prayer un-

[32]Reading with Tehran edition, *raqim,* for Dabir-Siyāqi's edition, *rasim.* The "Lords of al-Raqim" are mentioned in passing in Koran 18:9.

til the next evening, as in the month of Ramadān, although they do eat dates during the day. I saw excellent dates there, much better than in Basra and other places. These people are extremely poverty stricken and destitute; nonetheless, they spend the whole day fighting and killing each other. They have a kind of date called *maydun* that weighs ten dirhems, the pit weighing not more than ½ dānaks. They claimed that this particular date could be kept for twenty years without spoilage. Their currency is Nishapuri gold.

I stayed four months in this Falaj under the worst possible conditions: nothing of this world remained in my possession except two satchels of books, and they were a hungry, naked, and ignorant people. Everyone who came to pray brought his sword and shield with him as a matter of course. They had no reason to buy books.

There was a mosque in which we stayed. I had a little red and blue paint with me, so I wrote a line of poetry on the wall and drew a branch with leaves up through the writing. When they saw it, they were amazed, and everybody in the compound gathered around to look at what I had done. They told me that if I would paint the *mehrāb* they would give me one hundred maunds of dates. Now a hundred maunds of dates was a fortune for them. Once while I was there, a company of Arab soldiers came and demanded five hundred maunds of dates. They refused to give it and fought, which resulted in the death of ten people from the compound. A thousand palms were cut down, but they did not give up even ten maunds of dates. Therefore, when they offered me that much, I painted the *mehrāb*, and that hundred maunds of dates was an answer to our prayers, since we had not been able to obtain any food.

We had almost given up hope of ever being able to get out of that desert, the nearest trace of civilization in any direction being two hundred parasangs away through fearful, devastating desert. In all those four months, I never saw five maunds of wheat in one place. Finally, however, a caravan came from Yamāma to take goat's leather to Lahsā. Goat's leather is brought from the Yemen via Falaj and sold to merchants. An Arab offered to take me to Basra, but I had no money to pay the fare. It is only two hundred parasangs to Basra from there, and the hire for a camel was one dinar, whereas a good camel can be bought outright for two or three dinars. Since I had no cash with me, they took me on credit on condition that I pay thirty dinars in Basra. I was forced to agree to these terms, although I had never in my life so much as set foot in Basra!

The Arabs packed my books and seated my brother on a camel, and thus, with me on foot, we set out, headed toward the ascent of the Pleiades. The ground was flat, without so much as a mountain or hill, and wherever the earth was a bit harder, there was rainwater standing in pools. As these people travel night and day, without the slightest trace of a road visible, they must go by instinct. What is amazing is that with no indication or warning, suddenly they come upon a well.

To make a long story short, in four days and nights we came to Yamāma, which has inside a large, old fortress, and outside a town with a bazaar containing all sorts of artisans and a fine mosque. The emirs there are Alids of old, and no one has ever been able to wrest the region from their control, since, in the first place there is not, nor has there been, a conquering sultan or king anywhere near, and, in the second, those Alids possess such might that they can mount three to four hundred horsemen. They are of the Zaydi sect, and when they stand in prayer they say, "Mohammad and ʿAli are the best of mankind," and, "Come to the best deed!"[33] The inhabitants of this town are Sharifis, and they have running water, irrigation canals, and many palm groves in the district. They told me that when dates are plentiful, a thousand maunds are only one dinar.

It is forty parasangs from Yamāma to Lahsā. During the winter it is possible to travel because potable rainwater collects in pools, but not in summer.

A Description of Lahsā

To reach the town of Lahsā from any direction, you have to cross vast expanses of desert. The nearest Muslim city to Lahsā

[33]These words characterize the Shiʿite (including the Zaydi) call to prayer. The Sunni call to prayer includes neither phrase. In Nāṣer's terminology "Alid" (*ʿalawi*) refers to any of the Shiʿa, including (1) the Zaydis, followers of Zayd, son of the Fourth Imam ʿAli Zayn al-ʿĀbedin (d. 94/712): members of this sect ruled

that has a ruler is Basra, and that is one hundred and fifty parasangs away. There has never been a ruler of Basra, however, who has attempted an attack on Lahsā.

All of the town's outlying villages and dependencies are enclosed by four strong, concentric walls made of reinforced mud brick. The distance between these walls is about a parasang, and there are enormous wells inside the town, each the size of five millstones around. All the water of the district is put to use so that none goes outside the walls. A really splendid town is situated inside these fortifications, with all the appurtenances of a large city, and there are more than twenty thousand soldiers.

They said that the ruler had been a *sharif* who prevented the people from practicing Islam and relieved them of the obligations of prayer and the fast by claiming that he was the ultimate authority on such matters. His name was Abu Sa'id and when you ask the townspeople what sect they belong to, they say they are Busa'idis. They neither pray nor fast, but they do believe in Mohammad and his mission. Abu Sa'id told them that he would come among them again after his death, and his tomb, a fine shrine, is located inside the city. He directed that six of his [spiritual] sons[34] should maintain his rule with justice and equity and without dispute among themselves until he should come again. Now they have a palace that is the seat of state and a throne that accommodates all six kings in one place, and they rule in complete accord and harmony. They have also six viziers, and when the kings are all seated on their throne, the six viziers are seated opposite on another bench. Thus all affairs are handled in mutual consultation. At the time I was there they had thirty thousand Zanzibari and Abyssinian slaves working in the fields and gardens.

They take no tax from the peasantry, and whenever anyone is stricken by poverty or contracts a debt they take care of his needs until the debtor's affairs should be cleared up. And if any-

in Gilān, Daylam and Ṭabarestān in Iran from 864 to 1126 and founded a dynasty in the Yemen in 901; (2) Ismailis, who followed Esmā'il, son of the Sixth Imam Ja'far al-Ṣādeq (d. 148/765): to this sect belonged the Fatimids of Egypt; and (3) Twelvers (*ethnā'ashari*), who followed the lineal descent of imams from 'Ali until the Twelfth Imam Moḥammad al-Montaẓar (ca. 264/878).

[34]Cf. Bernard Lewis, *The Origins of Ismā'īlism* (Cambridge: Cambridge University Press, 1944), p. 99, n. 5, who translates "disciples" for "sons."

one is in debt to another, the creditor cannot claim more than the amount of the debt. Any stranger to the city who possesses a craft by which to earn his livelihood is given enough money to buy the tools of his trade and establish himself, when he repays however much he was given. If anyone's property or implements suffer loss and the owner is unable to undertake necessary repairs, they appoint their own slaves to make the repairs and charge the owner nothing. The rulers have several gristmills in Lahsā where the citizenry can have their meal ground into flour for free, and the maintenance of the buildings and the wages of the miller are paid by the rulers. The rulers are called simply "lord" and the viziers, "counsel."

There was once no Friday mosque in Lahsā, and the sermon and congregational prayer were not held. A Persian man, however, named ʿAli son of Ahmad, who was a Muslim, a pilgrim and very wealthy, did build a mosque in order to provide for pilgrims who arrived in the city.

Their commercial transactions are carried out in lead [tokens], which are kept in wrappers, each of which is equivalent to six thousand dirhem-weights. When paying for something, they do not even count out the wrappers but take them as they are. No one takes this currency outside, however. They also weave fine scarves that are exported to Basra and other places.

They do not prevent anyone from performing prayers, although they themselves do not pray. The ruler answers most politely and humbly anyone who speaks to him, and wine is not indulged in.

A horse outfitted with collar and crown is kept always tied close by the tomb of Abu Saʿid, and a watch is continually maintained day and night for such time as he should rise again and mount the horse. Abu Saʿid said to his sons, "When I come again among you, you will not recognize me. The sign will be that you strike my neck with my sword. If it be me, I will immediately come back to life." He made this stipulation so that no one else could claim to be him.

In the time of the Baghdad caliphs one of the rulers attacked Mecca and killed a number of people who were circumambulating the Kaʿba at the time. They removed the Black Stone from its corner and took it to Lahsā. They said that the stone was a "human magnet" that attracted people, not knowing that it was the nobility and magnificence of Mohammad that drew people there, for the Stone had lain there for long ages without anyone paying any particular attention to it. In the end, the Black Stone was bought back and returned to its place.

In the city of Lahsā they sell all kinds of animals for meat, such as dog, cat, donkey, cow, sheep, and so on, and the head and skin of whatever animal it is is placed next to the meat so that the customer will know what he is buying. They fatten up dogs, just like grazed sheep, until they are too heavy to walk, after which they are slaughtered and eaten.

Seven parasangs east of Lahsā is the sea. In this sea is the island of Bahrain, which is fifteen parasangs long. There is a large city there and many palm groves. Pearls are found in the sea thereabouts, and half of the divers' take belongs to the sultan of Lahsā. South of Lahsā is Oman, which is on the Arabian peninsula, but three sides face desert that is impossible to cross. The region of Oman is eighty parasangs square and tropical; there they grow coconuts, which they call *nārgil.* Directly east of Oman across the sea are Kish and Mokrān. South of Oman is Aden, while in the other direction is the province of Fārs.

There are so many dates in Lahsā that animals are fattened on them and at times more than one thousand maunds are sold for one dinar. Seven parasangs north of Lahsā is a region called Qatif, where there is also a large town and many date-palms. An Arab emir from there once attacked Lahsā, where he maintained seige for a year. One of those fortification walls he captured and wrought much havoc, although he did not obtain much of anything. When he saw me, he asked whether or not it was in the stars for him to take Lahsā, as they were irreligious. I told him what was expedient [for me to say], since, in my opinion also, the bedouins and people of Lahsā were as close as anyone could be to irreligiosity, there being people there who, from one year to the next, never perform ritual ablutions. This that I record is told from my own experience and not from false rumors, since I was there among them for nine consecutive months, and not at intervals.

I was unable to drink their milk, and whenever I asked for water to drink they offered me milk instead. As I did not take the proffered milk and asked for water, they would say, "Wherever you see water, ask for it there!" In all their lives they had never seen a bath or running water.

Now let me return to my story. Having set out for Basra from Yamāma, we encountered some way stations with water and others with no water. On the 20th of Shaʿbān 443 [27 December 1051] we arrived in Basra.

A Description of the City of Basra

The city has a large wall, except for the portion that faces the water, where there is no wall. The water here is all marsh, the Tigris and Euphrates coming together at the beginning of the Basra district, and when the water of the Hawiza[35] joins the confluence, it is called Shatt al-ʿArab. From this Shatt al-ʿArab, two large channels have been cut, between the mouths of which is a distance of one parasang, running in the direction of the *qebla* for four parasangs, after which they converge and run another one parasang to the south. From these channels numerous canals have been dug in all directions among palm groves and orchards. Of these two channels, the higher one, which is northeast, is called Nahr Maʿqel, whereas the southwestern one is called Nahr Obolla. These two channels form an enormous rectangular "island," on the shortest side of which Basra is situated. To the southwest of Basra is open plain that supports neither settlement nor agriculture.

When I arrived, most of the city lay in ruins, the inhabited parts being greatly dispersed, with up to half a parasang from one quarter to another. Nonetheless, the walls were strong and well kept, the populace numerous, and the ruler with plenty of income. At that time, the emir of Basra was the son of Abā Kālijār the Daylamite, king of Fārs. His vizier was a Persian, Abu Mansur Shāhmardān by name.

Every day there are three bazaars in Basra: in the morning transactions are held at a place called Suq al-Khozāʿa [Market of the Khozāʿa Tribe]; in the middle of the day at Suq ʿOthmān

[35]Ḥawiza with Berlin edition for Tehran and Dabir-Siyāqi's edition's Jubara.

[ʿOthman's Market]; and at the end of the day at Suq al-Qaddāhin [Flintmakers Market]. The procedure at the bazaar is as follows: you turn over whatever you have to a moneychanger and get in return a draft; then you buy whatever you need, deducting the price from the moneychanger's draft. No matter how long one might stay in the city, one would never need anything more than a moneychanger's draft.

When we arrived we were as naked and destitute as madmen, for it had been three months since we had unloosed our hair. I wanted to enter a bath in order to get warm, the weather being chilly and our clothing scant. My brother and I were clad only in old lungis with a piece of coarse fabric on our backs to keep out the cold. "In this state who would let us into a bath?" I asked. Therefore, I sold a small satchel in which I kept my books and wrapped the few rusty dirhems I had received in a piece of paper to give the bath attendant, thinking that he might give us a little while longer in the bath in order for us to remove the grime from our bodies. When I handed him the change, he looked at us as though we were madmen and said, "Get away from here! People are coming out of the bath." As he would not allow us in, we came away humiliated and in haste. Even the children who were playing at the bathhouse door thought we were madmen and, throwing stones and yelling, chased after us. We retired into a corner and reflected in amazement on the state of the world.

Now, as we were in debt to the camel driver for thirty dinars, we had no recourse save the vizier of the king of Ahwāz, Abu'l-Fath ʿAli son of Ahmad, a worthy man, learned in poetry and *belles-lettres*, and very generous, who had come to Basra with his sons and retinue and taken up residence but who, at present, had no administrative position. Therefore, I got in touch with a Persian, also a man of learning, with whom I had some acquaintance and who had entree to the vizier but who was also in straightened circumstances and totally without means to be of assistance to me. He mentioned my situation to the vizier, who, as soon as he heard, sent a man with a horse for me to come to him just as I was. Too ashamed of my destitution and nakedness, I hardly thought it fitting to appear before him, so I wrote a note of regret, saying that I would come to him later. I had two reasons for doing this: one was my poverty, and the other was,

Persian Gulf area

as I said to myself, that he now imagines that I have some claim to being learned, but when he sees my note he will figure out just what my worth is so that when I go before him I need not be ashamed.

Immediately he sent me thirty dinars to have a suit of clothing made. With that amount I bought two fine suits and on the third day appeared at the vizier's assembly. I found him to be a worthy, polite, and scholarly man of pleasant appearance, humble, religious, and well spoken. He had four sons, the eldest of whom was an eloquent, polite, and reasonable youth called Ra'is Abu ʿAbd Allāh Ahmad son of ʿAli son of Ahmad. Not only a poet and administrator, he was wise and devout beyond his youthful age. We were taken in and stayed there from the first of Shaʿbān until the middle of Ramadān. The thirty dinars due the Arab for our camel were paid by the vizier, and I was relieved of that burden. (May God thus deliver all His servants from the torment of debt!)

When I desired to depart he sent me off by sea with gifts and bounteous good things so that I reached Fārs in ease and comfort, thanks to the generosity of that noble man. (May God delight in such noble men!)

In Basra there are thirteen shrines in the name of the Prince of the Faithful ʿAli son of Abu Tāleb, one of which is called the Banu Māzen Shrine. The Prince of the Faithful ʿAli came to Basra during Rabiʿ I in the year 36 [September 655], while ʿĀ'esha was waging war against him, and married Laylā, the daughter of Masʿud Nahshali. This shrine was the house of that lady, and the Prince of the Faithful stayed there for seventy-two days, after which he returned to Kufa. There is another shrine next to the cathedral mosque called the Bāb al-Tib Shrine.

Inside the cathedral mosque, I saw a wooden post thirty cubits long and five spans, four fingers thick, although it is somewhat thicker at one end. This post is from India and the Prince of the Faithful is said to have picked it up and brought it there. The other eleven shrines are in different places, and I visited them all.

After our worldly condition had taken a turn for the better and we each had on decent clothing, we went back one day to the bathhouse we had not been allowed to enter. As soon as we came through the door the attendant and everyone there stood up respectfully. We went inside, and the scrubber and servant came to attend to us. When we emerged from the bath all who were in the dressing room rose and remained standing until we had put on our clothes and departed. During that time the attendant had said to a friend of his, "These are those very young men whom we refused admission one day." They imagined that we did not know their language, but I said in Arabic, "You are perfectly correct. We are the very ones who had old sacks tied to our backs." The man was ashamed and most apologetic. Now these two events transpired within twenty days, and I have included the story so that men may know not to lament adversity brought on by fate and not to despair of the Creator's mercy, for He is merciful indeed.

A Description of the Ebb and Flow of the Tide at Basra

Every twenty-four hours the Sea of Oman flows twice, rising approximately ten ells. When high tide has been achieved it gradually ebbs, receding ten to twelve ells. The ten ells just mentioned can be seen either on a post erected at Basra or against the city walls. Where the ground is flat the tide covers an enormous area inland. The Tigris and Euphrates indeed flow so calmly that in places it cannot be determined which direction the water is flowing, and when the tide floods the river water rises for nearly forty parasangs, and one would think the flow had reversed itself and the water was backing up. In other places along the coast, however, the shore is relatively steep. Wherever the land is flat the water covers a large area, but wherever it is steep less ground is taken by the tide. They say that the ebb and flow of the tide are connected in some way to the moon because when the moon is at one of the nodes, which occurs on the tenth and [twenty] fourth [of the month], the flow is more; when the moon is on the east or west horizon, the ebb is maximum, and when the moon is in conjunction with or directly opposite the sun the flow is greatest and highest. During the quadratures it is the least, that is, the flow is not so great as during alignment with the sun, and the ebb is not so low as during alignment. For these reasons they say that the tides have something to do with the moon, but God knows best.

I found the town of Obolla, located by the channel named for it, to be populous, with more palaces, bazaars, mosques, and caravanserais than can be described. The original part of the town is to the north of the channel, although there are also quarters, mosques, caravanserais, and bazaars to the north. There are such pleasant edifices there as are to be found nowhere else in the world, and this section is called Shāte' ʿOthmān.

The large marsh formed by the Tigris and Euphrates and called Shatt al-ʿArab lies to the east of Obolla, the channel cutting across the south. The Obolla and Maʿqel Rivers join at Basra, as has already been stated.

Basra has twenty districts, each of which is comprised of villages and farms. The districts of Basra are as follows: Heshshān, Sharabba, Balās, ʿAqr [al-Sadan ?], Maysān, Nahr Harb, Shatt al-ʿArab, Saʿd [?], Salm [?], Jorayr, al-Mashān, al-Samd [?], al-Jawwith, Jazirat al-ʿOzma [?], Masroqānān, al-Sharir [?], Jazirat al-ʿOrsh al-Hamida [?], al-Howayza, al-Mofradāt [?].[36]

They say that once, at the mouth of the Obolla channel, there was a huge whirlpool that prevented boats from passing, but a wealthy lady of Basra had four hundred boats constructed and filled with date pits. The boats were then tightly sealed and sunk in the whirlpool, and now ships can sail through.

In short, the middle of Shawwāl 443 [February 1052] we left Basra by boat. For four parasangs out of Obolla there was on both sides of the channel an uninterrupted series of gardens, orchards, kiosks, and belvederes. Tributaries of the channel, each the size of a river, opened up on each side. When we reached Shāte' ʿOthmān we disembarked just opposite the city of Obolla and stayed a while.

[36]Some of these names have been verified in Yāqūt, *Moʿjam al-boldān*, ed. Ferdinand Wüstenfeld (Leipzig: Brockhaus, 1866–1870). They are as follows: Ḥeshshān (II, 272), Sharabba (III, 272), Balās (I, 708), ʿAqr (a ʿAqr al-Sadan is given in III, 697), Maysān (IV, 714), Maftaḥ (IV, 586), Nahr Ḥarb (IV, 838), Shaṭṭ al-ʿArab (not given in Yāqut but sufficiently well known), Jorayr (II, 68), al-Mashān (IV, 536), al-Jawwith (II, 163, with this reading for Dabir-Siyāqi's edition, al-Juna), Masroqānān (IV, 528, with this reading as suggested by Dabir-Siyāqi for his edition's Masarfāl), al-Ḥowayza (II, 371f.). The others (Saʿd, Salm, al-Ṣamd, Jazirat al-ʿOẓmā, al-Sharir, Jazirat al-ʿOrsh [perhaps al-Fors] al-Ḥamida [perhaps a separate name], and al-Mofradāt) have not been identified.

On the 17th we boarded a type of boat called *busi*, and great multitudes of people on either side called out, "O *busi*, may God speed you in safety!"

When we reached ʿAbbādān everyone got out of the boat. ʿAbbādān is a coastal town something like an island because the marsh splits in two there, and the only way to reach the town is by water. To the south is the sea itself, which, during high tide, reaches right up to the city walls; at low tide, however, the sea recedes a little less than two parasangs. Some of our party bought carpets in ʿAbbādān and others something to eat. The next morning the ship set out again toward the north. For ten parasangs the sea water was drinkable and good, since it was marsh water, the marsh flowing like a tongue out into the sea.

At dawn something like a small bird could be seen on the sea. The closer we approached the larger it appeared. When it was about one parasang to our left, an adverse wind came up so they dropped anchor and took down the sail. I asked what that thing was and was told that it was called a "*khashshāb*." It consisted of four enormous wooden posts made of teak and was shaped something like a war machine, squarish, wide at the base and narrow at the top. It was about forty ells above the surface of the water and had tile and stone on top held together by wood so as to form a kind of ceiling. On top of that were four arched openings where a sentinel could be stationed. Some said this *khashshāb* had been constructed by a rich merchant, others that a king had had it made. It served two functions: first, that area was being silted in and the sea consequently becoming shallow so that if a large ship chanced to pass, it would strike bottom. At night lamps encased in glass (so that the wind would not blow them out) were lit for people to see from afar and take precaution, since there was no possibility of rescue. Second, one could know the extent of the land and, if there were thieves, steer a ship away. When the *khashshāb* was no longer visible, another one of the same shape came into view; but this one did not have the watchtower on top, as though it had not been finished.[37]

[37]In his geography Abu'l-Fedā says: "To the south and east of ʿAbbādān are wooden [piles] (*khashabāt*), which are markers in the sea for boats to tie up to and not to go beyond lest the tide be low and they strike ground. At night fire is placed on these markers as a beacon for ships." Abu'l-Fedā, *Taqwim al-boldān*, ed. by Reinaud and MacGuckin de Slane (Paris: L'Imprimerie Royale, 1840), p. 309.

Next we came to Mahrubān, a large coastal town with a bazaar and fine mosque. Their only water is from rain, there being no freshwater wells or canals, although they have enough tanks and cisterns to insure an adequate supply. Three large caravanserais have been built there, each one as strong and as tall as a fortress. I saw the name of Yaʿqub son of Layth written on the pulpit of the Friday mosque and asked how this had come to be. They told me that Yaʿqub son of Layth had conquered up to this town but that no other emir of Khorasan had had the might to do it. When I was there, the town was in the hands of the sons of Abā Kālijār, the king of Fārs. Foodstuffs and commodities all have to be brought in from outside since there is nothing but fish in the town, which serves as a customs station and port.

South along the coast are Tavva and Kāzarun, but I remained in Mahrubān because they said the way was not safe, since the sons of Abā Kālijār had each rebelled against the other and had put the countryside into confusion. I was told that in Arrajān there was a great and learned man called Shaikh Sadid Mohammad son of ʿAbd al-Malek. When I heard this, since I was so weary of staying in that town, I wrote him a note explaining my situation and pleaded with him to get me out of there and into a safe place. Three days later thirty armed foot soldiers approached me and told me they had been sent by the shaikh to take me to Arrajān. Thus we were hospitably taken to Arrajān, a large town with a population of twenty thousand, to the east of which is a river that comes from the mountains. North of this river four large canals have been cut at great expense to bring water through the town and out the other side to where there are gardens and orchards of dates, oranges, citrons, and olives in abundance. The city is so constructed that for every house above ground there is also one below. Water flows through these basements and cellars so that during the summer they can be comfortable. The people there are of most every sect, and the Muʿtazilites have an imam called Abu Saʿid of Basra, an eloquent man with some claim to knowledge of geometry and mathematics. We held discussions together on dialectic theology and mathematics.

We left on the first of Moharram and headed for Isfahan via the mountains. Along the way we came to a mountain with a narrow pass, said by the common people to have been cut by Bahrām Gor with his sword. They call it Shamshir-borid ["Cut-by-Sword"]. There we saw a great stream that emerged on our right from a hole and then tumbled down a great height. The common people said that this water flows continuously during the summer but stops and freezes over during the winter months.

We reached Lurdajān, which is forty parasangs from Arrajān and which is the border of Fārs. From there we continued on to Khān Lanjān, where I noticed the name of Toghrel Beg inscribed over the gate. It was only seven parasangs from there to Isfahan, and the people of Khān Lanjān were remarkably safe and secure, everyone occupied with his own business.

On the 8th of Safar 444 [9 June 1052] we reached Isfahan. It is one hundred and eighty parasangs from Basra to Isfahan, a city located on a flat plain and with a delightful climate. Wherever one sinks a well ten ells into the ground, refreshing cold water comes out. The city has a high, strong wall with gates, embrasures, and battlements all around. Inside the city are courses for running water, fine tall buildings, and a beautiful and large Friday mosque. The city wall is said to be three and a half parasangs long, and everything inside is in a flourishing state, as I saw nothing in ruins. There were many bazaars; one that I saw was only for money changers and contained two hundred stalls. Every bazaar has doors and gates, as do all quarters and lanes. The caravanserais are exceptionally clean, and in one lane, called Ku-Tarāz, there were fifty fine caravanserais, in each of which were retail merchants and shopkeepers. The caravan we entered with had 1,300 *kharvārs* of goods, yet there was no difficulty in finding space since there seemed to be no lack of room or fodder.

When Sultan Toghrel Beg Abu Tāleb Mohammad son of Mikā'il son of Saljuq took the city, he appointed as governor a young Nishapuri, a good administrator with a fine hand, composed, well met, a patron of learning, well spoken, and generous, called Khwāja ʿAmid. The sultan ordered him not to levy taxes on the people for three years, and, as he followed this order, the peasantry that had fled returned home. He had been one of the bureaucrats serving under Suri.[38]

[38]Suri b. al-Moʿtazz, the chief of Khorasan under the Ghaznavid Masʿud, according to M. Dabir-Siyāqi in his second edition of the *Safarnāma* (Tehran, 1335/1957), p. 124, n. 1.

Before our arrival there had been a great famine, but by the time we came they were harvesting barley, and 1½ maunds of bread were selling for one dirhem, as were 3 maunds of barley bread. The people, however, were still complaining that never in this city had less than 8 maunds of bread been more than one dirhem. Of all the Persian-speaking cities, I never saw a finer, more commodious, or more flourishing city than Isfahan. They claimed that wheat, barley, and other grains could be left for twenty years without spoiling, although some said that before the walls had been built the air was even better than now and that it had changed with the construction of the wall so that some things would spoil. The villages, however, were said to be as good as ever.

As the caravan was not going to leave for some time, I remained in Isfahan for twenty days. On the 28th of Safar [29 June 1052] we departed and came to the village of Haythamābād. From there we reached Na'in via the desert and mountains of Maskinān, a distance of thirty parasangs. From Na'in we traveled forty-three parasangs to the village of Garma in the Biyābān district, which comprises some ten or twelve villages. It is warm there, and there are date trees. This region was formerly held by the Kufjān,[39] but when we passed through, the prince Gilaki had seized the region from them and had stationed a deputy in a small fortress in a village called Piyāda in order to control the area and keep the roads safe. Whenever the Kufjān attempted banditry, Prince Gilaki's cavalry were sent to capture and kill them. It was due to the maintenance of that prince the road was safe and the people secure. (May God keep just princes and have mercy on the souls of the departed!)

Every two parasangs along this Biyābān road, small towers with water tanks have been built to collect rainwater in places that are not brackish so that people will not lose their way and also so that travelers may stop off and rest for a while out of the heat and cold.

We saw great areas of shifting sands along the way. If anyone were to stray from the markers and wander into these shifting sands, there is no way he could come out again and he would surely perish. We continued past there, when brackish earth

[39]The "Kufjān" have been identified with certain Baluch tribes.

came into view, all pocked and pitted; this lasted for six parasangs. If anyone went off the path, he would sink in.

From there we went via the caravanserai of Zobayda, which is called Rebāt-e Marāmi. In that caravanserai are five wells. If it were not for that caravanserai and water no one would be able to cross this desert. After that we came to four villages in the district of Tabas, one of which is called Rostābād.

On the 9th of Rabiʿ I [9 July] we reached Tabas, which is one hundred and ten parasangs from Isfahan. Although it looks like a village, Tabas is actually large, but water is scarce and agriculture minimal, with the exception of date palms and orchards. Nishapur lies forty parasangs north, and a like distance south across the desert is Khabis, while there are forbidding mountains to the east. At that time, the prince of the city was Gilaki son of Mohammad, who had taken it by the sword. The people were so secure that at night they did not lock their doors and even left their animals in the streets, despite the fact that there was no city wall. No woman dared speak to a stranger, for if she did they would both be killed. On account of this prince's protection and justice there was neither thief nor murderer.

Among the Arabs and Persians I saw four places remarkable for their security and justice: one, the region of Dasht during the reign of Lashkar Khan; two, in Daylamestān under the Amir-Amirān Jostān son of Ebrāhim; three, Egypt during the reign of al Mostanser be'llāh, Prince of the Faithful, and four, in Tabas during the reign of Prince Abu'l Hasan Gilaki son of Mohammad. In all my travels I never saw or heard of any place so secure as these four.

[The prince] kept us in Tabas for seventeen days and showed us much hospitality. When we left he bestowed presents and apologized for any shortcomings. (May God rejoice in him!) He sent one of his equerries along with me as far as Zuzan, which is seventy-two parasangs away. Twelve parasangs from Tabas we came upon a town called Raqqa, which had running water, farms, gardens, trees, walls, a Friday mosque, and villages and agricultural dependencies.

On the 9th of Rabiʿ II [8 August] we left Raqqa and on the 12th arrived in Tun, twenty parasangs distant. The city of Tun had once been large, but when I passed through, most of it had fallen to ruin. Although it is on the edge of the desert, it has run-

Eastern Iran and northern Afghanistan

ning water, canals, and many gardens on the eastern side. It has also a strong fortress, and there are said to have been four hundred workshops where rugs were woven. There were many pistachio trees inside the houses, although the people of Balkh and Tokharestān imagine that pistachios grow only on mountains.

After leaving Tun, [Prince] Gilaki's man told me that once they had been traveling between Tun and Gonābedh when a band of thieves attacked. Out of fear, several people threw themselves down a canal well. One of them had a kindly father who came and hired someone to go down into the well and bring out the body of his son. They collected all the rope they had while lots of others gathered around to watch. Seven hundred ells of rope went down before that fellow reached the bottom. He tied the rope around the son's dead body and they hauled him out. When he came back up he said that a great amount of water was flowing through the canal, which goes for four parasangs and is said to have been built by Kay Khosraw.

On the 23rd of Rabiʿ II [22 August] we came to Qāʾen, said to be a distance of eighteen parasangs from Tun, although a caravan can make it in four days, so the estimate must be too great.

Qāʾen is a large fortified town, and all around the main city is a trench. The Friday mosque is also in the main city and has a huge arch where the *maqsura* is located. This arch is much larger than any I have seen in Khorasan, but it is not in proportion to the mosque. All buildings in the city are domed.

Eighteen parasangs northeast of Qāʾen is Zuzan. South to Herat is thirty parasangs.

In Qāʾen I saw a man named Abu Mansur Mohammad son of Dost, who knew something of medicine, astronomy, and logic.

"Outside the celestial spheres and stars, what is there?" he asked me.

"Things that are inside the spheres have names," I said, "but not anything outside them."

"What say you then?" he asked, "Is there substance outside the spheres or not?"

"The universe must of necessity be finite," I said. "And its limit is the last sphere. Indeed, it is called 'limit' precisely because there is nothing on the other side. When this limit has been realized, it then becomes necessary that what is outside the spheres not be like what is inside them."

"Therefore," he continued, "that substance, which reason must hold to be existent, is finite and ends at that limit. If it then be finite, up to what point does it exist? If it is infinite and without end, how then can it ever pass out of existence?" He went on in this manner and finally said, "I have suffered much perplexity over all this."

"Who hasn't?" I replied.

In short, because of the disturbances in Zuzan occasioned by ʿObayd of Nishapur and the rebellion of the head of Zuzan, I stayed one month in Qāʾen after I had sent Prince Gilaki's equerry back to him.

From Qāʾen we came to Sarakhs on the 2nd of Jomādā II [29 September 1052]. From Basra to Sarakhs I reckoned the distance to be 390 parasangs. From Sarakhs we went via the caravanserais of Jaʿfari, ʿAmravi, and Neʿmati, all three of which are close together on the road. On the 12th of Jomādā II [19 October] we reached Marv Rud. Two days later we left and passed through Ābgarm. On the 19th we came to Bāryāb, a distance of 36 parasangs.

The prince of Khorasan, Chaghri Bēg Abu Solaymān Dāud son of Mikā'il son of Saljuq was in Shoburghān, headed for Marv, his capital. Because of the unsafe road, we went toward Samangān and thence by way of Seh Darra toward Balkh. When we reached the caravanserai of Seh Darra, we heard that my brother Khwāja Abu 'l-Fath ʿAbd al-Jalil was in the entourage of the prince of Khorasan's vizier, Abu Nasr. Now it had been seven years since I had left Khorasan. When we reached Dastgerd, I saw loads being taken toward Shoburghān. My brother, who was with me, asked who these goods belonged to and was told that they were the vizier's.

"Do you know Abu'l-Fath ʿAbd al-Jalil?" he asked.

"One of his men is with us," they said. And immediately a man came to us and asked where we were coming from.

"From the Pilgrimage," we answered.

"My master, Abu'l-Fath ʿAbd al-Jalil, had two brothers," he said, "who went on the Pilgrimage many years ago, and he still longs to see them, but no one he has questioned has had any news of them."

"We have a letter from Nāser," my brother said. "When your master comes, we will give it to him." A moment later, however, the caravan began to move, and we started to join it.

"My master is coming just now," said the fellow, "and if he misses you, he will be disappointed. Why don't you give me the letter so I can give it to him and make him happy?"

"Would you rather have Nāser's letter," asked my brother, "or Nāser himself—for here he is!" And the fellow was so overjoyed he did not know what to do. Thereupon we set out for Balkh by way of Miyān Rustā. Meanwhile, my brother Khwāja Abu'l-Fath had gone to Dastgerd by way of Dasht and was accompanying the prince of Khorasan's vizier. When he heard of us he returned from Dastgerd and waited for us at the Jomukiān Bridge.

On Tuesday the 26th of Jomādā II 444 [23 October 1052], after having had little or no hope and having at times fallen into perilous circumstances and having even despaired of our lives, we were all together again and joyful to see each other. We thanked God for that, and on that same day we arrived in Balkh, wherefore I composed these lines of poetry:

'Though the toil and travail of the world be long
An end will doubtless come to good and bad.
The spheres travel for us day and night:
Whatever has once gone, another comes on its heels.
We are traveling through what can be passed
Until there comes that journey that cannot be bypassed.

The distance we traversed from Balkh to Egypt and thence to Mecca and then via Basra to Fārs and finally back to Balkh, not counting excursions for visiting shrines and so on was 2,220 parasangs. I have recorded my adventures as I saw them. If some of what I heard narrated by others does not conform to the truth, I beg my readers to forgive me and not to reproach me. If God grants me success in making a journey to the East, what I may see will be appended hereto, if God the One wills.

Praise be to God, the Lord of the Universe, and prayers be upon Mohammad and his House and Companions all!

Glossary of Persons

Abā Kālijār ʿEmād al-Din Marzobān (r. 415–40/1024–28). Buwayhid prince, ruled Fārs and Khuzestān from Shiraz. See EI^2, I, 131f.

ʿAbd Allāh b. ʿAbbās (d. 68/686): known as the father of Koranic exegesis, one of the first to begin scholarly collections of Prophetic oral material and to engage in Koranic interpretation.

Abu Faḍl Khalifa: a native of Darband whom Nāṣer met in Shamirān.

Abu Hurayra (d. ca. 58/678): originally from the Yemen, a contemporary of the Prophet who narrated copious *ḥadith*. He is especially renowned for his piety.

Abu Jahl: one of the Prophet's most notorious rivals in Mecca, he was alleged even to have plotted an assassination attempt against the Prophet and later became proverbial as a godless opponent of righteousness.

Abu'l-ʿAlā' al-Maʿarri (363–449/973–1057): Syrian poet and litterateur noted for his asceticism and pessimistic view of humanity. He remains one of the finest Arabic poets and thinkers.

Abu'l-Fatḥ ʿAli b. Aḥmad: vizier to the king of Ahwāz according to Nāṣer, who met him in retirement in Basra in 443/1051. He may have been a vizier to Abā Kālijār or to one of his sons, Abu Manṣur Fulādsotun or al-Malek al-Raḥim Khosrawfērōz.

Abu'l-Ḥasan Gilaki b. Moḥammad: ruler of Ṭabas in 444/1052 when Nāṣer passed through. His son, ʿAlā' al-Molk Esmāʿil b. Gilaki, was a well-known Ismaili prince in Qohestān.

Abu Manṣur Vahsudān b. Mamlān (r. 416–51/1025–29): Ravvadid ruler of Azerbaijan at Tabriz.

Abu Saʿid al-Ḥasan al-Jannābi al-Laḥsāwi (d. 301/913): Ismaili *dāʿi* (missionary) of Ḥamdān Qarmaṭ in eastern Arabia; he built up the Qarmaṭi (Carmathian) state in Bahrain, 281–300/894–913.

Abu Solaymān Chaghri Bēg Dāud (ca. 380–452/990–1060): brother of the Seljuk Ṭoghrel Bēg, in charge of the Seljuk forces that took Marv in 423/1036 and, for a time, ruler of Khorasan. See EI^2, II, 4f.

ʿAli Nasā'i, Abu'l-Ḥasan, known as al-Ḥakim al-Mokhtaṣṣ: philosopher, mathematician and astronomer who was acquainted with both Avicenna and al-Biruni.

ʿAmr b. al-ʿĀṣ al-Sahmi (ca. 570–42/663): military commander under whom the Muslim forces conquered Egypt.

Bahrām Gōr: historically the Sasanian emperor Varahrān V (r. 421–39), his feats of prowess connect him with the ancient cult of

Heracles. In legendary guise he is the hero of Neẓāmi of Ganja's romance *Haft paykar*.

Bāyazid Besṭāmi, Ṭayfur b. ʿIsā (d. 261/874 or 264/877): great mystic noted especially for his ecstatic utterances.

Belāl the Abyssinian, Abu ʿAbd Allāh b. Rehāḥ (d. 25/645): a Companion to the Prophet and known for being the first muezzin in Islam.

Daqiqi, Abu Manṣur Moḥammad b. Aḥmad (d. ca. 980): early Persian poet at the Samanid and Chaghanian courts.

Dhu'l-Kefl: said variously to have been the name of Job's son or of a pious Israelite who resisted Satan's temptations. He is mentioned in the Koran, 21:85 and 38:48.

Ebn Abi ʿAqil: a Sunni *qāḍi* (judge) whom Nāṣer met in Tyre.

Fāṭema Zahrā: sole surviving daughter of the Prophet and wife of ʿAli b. Abi Ṭāleb, venerated by Shiʿites as the mother of the imams, the lineal descendants of the Prophet through her. The Fatimid dynasty was named after her.

al-Ḥākem be-Amr Allāh (r. 386–411/996–1021): Fatimid sultan of Egypt.

Ḥamza b. ʿAbd al-Moṭṭaleb (d. 625): paternal uncle of the Prophet who became a legendary figure renowned for fantastic exploits and great prowess. His adventures, which bear no relation to the historical person, are recorded in the popular Arabic *Sirat Amir Ḥamza* and in Persian romances under the name *Ḥamzanāma*.

Hud: a South Arabian prophet who was sent as an apostle to the tribe of ʿAd (see Koran 7:63).

Jostān II b. Ebrāhim, Abu Ṣāleḥ: the sixth Mosaferid/Kangarid ruler of Daylam and Azerbaijan. He was reigning in 437/1045.

Lashkar Khan: according to Nāṣer, ruler of Dasht. Neither the person nor the place has been identified.

Mahdi, al-, ʿObayd Allāh (r. 297–322/909–34 from North Africa): the first Fatimid caliph.

Maḥmud (r. 388–421/998–1030): Ghaznavid sultan.

Ma'mun, al- (r. 198–218/813–33): Abbasid caliph.

Manjik, Abu'l-Ḥasan ʿAli Termedhi: 10th-century poet at the Chaghanian court.

Masʿud (r. 421–32/1030–42): Ghaznavid sultan.

Mas'ud Nahshali: father of Laylā, a wife of 'Ali b. Abi Ṭāleb.

Mo'āwiya b. Abi Sofyān (r. 41–60/661–80): the first Umayyad caliph.

Mo'ezz le-Din Allāh, al- (r. 341–65/953–75): Fatimid sultan of Egypt.

Mostanṣer be'llāh, al- (r. 427–87/1036–94): Fatimid sultan of Egypt.

Mowaffaq, Khwaja, Hebat Allāh b. Moḥammad b. Ḥosayn: a member of the elite of Nishapur. It was he who handed the city over to Ṭoghrel Bēg's brother Yanāl at the Seljuk conquest. He was expelled from the city when it was reconquered by the Ghaznavids.

Naṣr al-Dawla Aḥmad, Abu Naṣr (r. 401–53/1011–61): Marwanid prince of eastern Anatolia at Diyār Bakr.

'Obayd Nishāpuri: according to Nāṣer, the ruler of Zuzan at the time he passed through in 444/1052.

Oways Qarani: a contemporary of the Prophet and native of the Yemen. A model of ascetic piety for later generations, he is said to have pulled out all his teeth in commemoration of a tooth lost by the Prophet at the Battle of Oḥod.

Pesar-e Shāddel: according to Nāṣer, a prince of Aden.

Qaṭrān, Abu Mansur, 'Aḍodi Tabrizi (d. 465/1072): said to have been the first poet of Azerbaijan to compose in Dari Persian.

Ṣāleḥ: a pre-Islamic prophet to the South Arabian tribe of Thamud. He is mentioned in the Koran, 7:71.

Suri, Abu'l-Faḍl, b. al-Mo'tazz: governor of Khorasan from Nishapur under the Ghaznavids Maḥmud and Mas'ud.

Ṭoghrel Bēg, Rokn al-Din Moḥammad b. Mikā'il (r. 429–55/1038–63): Seljuk ruler and conqueror.

Ya'qub b. Layth (r. 253–65/867–79): Saffarid ruler of Sistān.

Glossary of Places

Anglicized names are given in italics; others are transliterated. The provinces in which the towns and cities are placed by medieval geographers are given in parentheses. Variants, mainly arabizations, are also given.

ʿAbbādān (Iraq): the modern Iranian town of Abadan. See Yāqut, III, 597; Abu'l-Fedā, 308.

Ābgarm: said by Nāṣer to be a village between Marv Rud and Fāryāb; not located in the geographies.

Ābkhwari: said by Nāṣer to be a village between Dāmghān and Semnān. There is today a ruined village east of Dāmghān called Ābkhwārān, undoubtedly the same. See Dabir-Siyāqi, p. 193.

Acre, ʿAkkā (Syria): see Yāqut, III, 704; Abu'l-Fedā, 242.

Aden, ʿAdan (Yemen): the modern town and region on the southwestern coast of the Arabian peninsula. See Yāqut, III, 616; Abu'l-Fedā, 93.

Ahwāz (Khuzestān): the modern Iranian town. See Yāgut, I, 410; Abu'l-Fedā, 316.

Akhlāṭ (Armenia): the Ahlat of modern Turkey. See Yāqut, III, 457; Abu'l-Fedā, 394.

Akhmim, Ekhmim (Upper Egypt): the ancient Panopolis. See Yāqut, I, 165; Abu'l-Fedā, 110.

Aleppo, Ḥalab (Syria): the modern city. See Yāqut, II, 304; Abu'l-Fedā, 266.

Āmed (Mesopotamia, dependency of Diyār Bakr): ancient Amida. See Yāqut, I, 66; Abu'l-Fedā, 286. Āmed is the modern city of Diyarbekir in Turkey.

Āmol (Ṭabarestān): the modern Iranian city on the Caspian. See Yāqut, I, 68; Abu'l-Fedā, 434.

Antioch, Anṭākyā (Syria): see Yāqut, I, 382; Abu'l-Fedā, 256.

ʿArafāt: the mountain near Mecca. See Yāqut, III, 645.

ʿArʿar: a village said by Nāṣer to be three days distant from Jerusalem in the direction of Wādi al-Qorā. Yāqut, III, 645, says that there are several places named ʿArʿar and ʿUrāʿir but does not locate them precisely. LeStrange, p. 58, suggests that this is probably Aroer (ʿArōʿer) on the Arnon. Hütteroth and Abdulfattah, 159, give a village named ʿArʿarā, but it is in the wrong direction from Jerusalem.

Arragān, Arrajān (Khuzestān, on the Fārs border): see Yāqut, I, 193; Abu'l-Fedā, 318.

Arzan (Armenia): a town three days distant from Akhlāṭ. See Yāqut, I, 205; Abu'l-Fedā, 394.

Ascalon, ʿAsqalān (Palestine): a major town on the Mediterranean, not far from Gaza. See Yāqut, III, 673; Abu'l-Fedā, 238.

Aswān (Upper Egypt): same as modern town. See Yāqut, I, 269; Abu'l-Fedā, 112.

Asyuṭ (Upper Egypt, ancient Lycopolis): same as modern town. See Yāqut, I, 272; Abu'l-Fedā, 112.

ʿAthr (Yemen): see Yāqut, III, 615.

ʿAydhāb (Upper Egypt, Bāja region): see Yāqut, III, 751; Abu'l-Fedā, 23, 120.

Baḥr al-Naʿām (Upper Egypt, Red Sea coast): not mentioned in the geographies.

Balkh (Khorasan): see Yāqut, I, 713; Abu'l-Fedā, 460.

Baraz al-Khayr (?): no such name listed by geographers. Dabir-Siyāqi suggests that it is perhaps a scribal corruption of Borz-anjir or Bard-anjir. The town of Barzanj (Yāqut, I, 562), twelve parasangs from Bardhaʿa en route to Bāb al-Abwāb (Darband), is a likely possibility since Nāṣer mentions it as being between Qazvin and Shamirān.

Bargri, Bāgri, Bergri (Armenia, modern Muradiye): see Abu'l-Fedā, 389.

Bāryāb, same as Fāryāb, q.v.

Basra (Iraq, West Tigris and East Obolla): same as the modern Iraqi town. See Yāqut, I, 636; Abu'l-Fedā, 308.

Beirut, Bayrut (Syria): same as the modern Lebanese city. See Yāqut, I, 785; Abu'l-Fedā, 246.

Berwa, al- (Palestine): text has Barda, in error. The tombs of Esau and Simon are located here by Nāṣer. See Hütteroth and Abdulfattah, 190.

Besṭām, Basṭām (Ṭabarestān, Qumes): see Yāqut, I, 623: Abul'l-Fedā, 436.

Bethlehem, Bayt Laḥm (Palestine): see Yāqut, I, 779; Abu'l-Fedā, 241.

Beṭlis, Bedlis (Armenia): between Mayyāfāreqin and Akhlāṭ. See Yāqut, I, 526; Abu'l-Fedā, 394.

Bil: Yāqut, I, 798, gives two villages by this name, one near Rayy and the other near Sarakhs. Nāṣer lists it near Qazvin.

Bisha (Yemen): see Yāqut, I, 791.

Borqa (Arabia): area near Medina. See Yāqut, I, 575.

Byblos, Jobayl (Syria): the modern Lebanese town of Jubeil. See Yāqut, II, 32.

Caesarea, Qaysāriyya (Palestine): see Yāqut, IV, 214; Abu'l-Fedā, 238.

Cairo, al-Qāhera (Egypt): Old Cairo (Fosṭāṭ, see Yāqut, III, 893) was the site of the earliest Muslim garrison, dating from the Muslim conquest of Egypt; New Cairo (al-Qāhera, see Yāqut, IV, 22) was founded in 358/969 when the Fatimids conquered Egypt and established their capital there.

Chāshtkhwārān (Qumes): a village between Dāmghān and Semnān; today it is a field in Semnān, seven miles from Ahuān. See Dabir-Siyāqi, 227.

Damascus, Demashq al-Shām (Syria): the modern Syrian city. See Yāqut, II, 587; Abu'l-Fedā, 252.

Dāmghān (Ṭabarestān): chief town in the Qumes region. See Yāqut, II, 539; Abu'l-Fedā, 436.

Dammun (Palestine): Nāṣer gives this as the name of a village between Tyre and Irbid. Hütteroth and Abdulfattah, 193, give a village named Dāmun in the Acre region. See also Le Strange, 14, where it is also called Dāmun.

Darband, Bāb al-Abwāb (Azerbaijan): a town on the Caspian. See Abu'l-Fedā, 404.

Dasht: Nāṣer mentions Dasht twice, once as a village near Dastgerd and again as a place remarkable for security under the rule of Lashkar Khan. Yāqut, II, 575f., gives several places named Dasht: (1) a village near Isfahan, (2) a small town in Jebāl between Erbel (near Mosul) and Tabriz, (3) Dasht al-Arzan in Fārs, and (4) Dasht Bārin, a city in Fārs.

Dastgerd, Dastajerd (Khorasan): also known as Dastgerd Jomukiyān. See Yāqut, II, 573.

Ḍayqa, al- (Upper Egypt): a station ten parasangs from ʿAydhāb. See Yāqut, III, 484.

Diyār Bakr (Eastern Anatolia): the upper Tigris region. See Yāqut, II, 636.

Eʿbellin (?, Palestine): Nāṣer says it is a village between Acre and Irbid. No further identification has been made.

ʿErqa (Syria): a small town four parasangs east of Tripoli. See Yāqut, III, 653; Abu'l-Fedā, 254.

Falaj, Falj, Aflaj (Arabia): a place on the road between Basra and Yamāma. See Yāqut, III, 910.

Fāryāb, Bāryāb (Khorasan, Juzjān): a district and town near Balkh. See Yāqut, III, 840; Abu'l-Fedā, 460.

Gavān, Jovayn (Khorasan): a district between Besṭām and Nishapur. See Yāqut, II, 162; Abu'l-Fedā, 442.

Gonābedh, Jonābedh (Khorasan): a dependency of Nishapur, the modern Gonābād in Khorasan. See Yāqut, II, 120.

Haifa, Ḥayfā (Palestine): see Yāqut, II, 381.

Ḥamā (Syria): ancient Hamath, Epiphania. Same as the modern Syrian town. See Yāqut, II, 330; Abu'l-Fedā, 262.

Hamadān, Hamadhān (Jabal): the modern Iranian city. See Yāqut, IV, 981; Abu'l-Fedā, 416.

Ḥarrān (Mesopotamia, Diyār Bakr): same as the modern Turkish town of Harran. See Yāqut, II, 231; Abu'l-Fedā, 276.

Ḥawḍ: Nāṣer names this as a place in Upper Egypt. It has not been identified in the geographies.

Haythamābād: a village outside of Isfahan. See Yāqut, IV, 998.

Ḥaẓira: Nāṣer places it between Tyre and Irbid; not further identified.

Hebron, Bayt Ḥabrun, al-Khalil (Palestine): see Yāqut, II, 194 and 468; Abu'l-Fedā, 240.

Homs, Ḥemṣ (Syria): the modern Syrian town. See Yāqut, II, 334; Abu'l-Fedā, 260.

Irbid, Erbed, Arbad (Syria, Jordan): the ancient Arbela. The text has Erbel, perhaps an alternative form. The modern town of Irbid is in Jordan near Tiberias. See Yāqut, I, 184, where Irbid is said to contain the tombs of Moses's mother and four of Jacob's sons, Dan, Issachar, Zebulun, and Gad. See also Hütteroth and Abdulfattah, 203.

Jār, al- (Arabia, dependency of Medina): see Yāqut, II, 5; Abu'l-Fedā, 82.

Jazʿ (Arabia, east of Ṭāʿef): see Yāqut, II, 71.

Jidda, Jodda (Arabia, Hejaz): see Abu'l-Fedā, 92.

Jeʿrāna, al- (Arabia): see Yāqut, II, 85.

Joḥfa, al-: the *miqāt* for Egyptian pilgrims. See Yāqut, II, 35; Abu'l-Fedā, 80.

Juzjānān (Khorasan): see Yāqut, II, 149; Abu'l-Fedā, 446.

Kafr Kannā (Palestine): a village near Tiberias. See Yāqut, IV, 290; Hütteroth and Abdulfattah, 187.

Kafr Sābā (Palestine): a village in the Nablus district. See Yāqut, IV, 288; Hütteroth and Abdulfattah, 140.

Kafr Sallām (Palestine): a village between Caesarea and Nablus. See Yāqut, IV, 288.

Kafr Ṭāb (Syria, Jond Ḥemṣ): a town between Aleppo and Maʿarrat al-Noʿmān. See Yāqut, IV, 289; Abu'l-Fedā, 262. Text has "Koway-māt," a scribal error.

Kanisa (?, Palestine): Nāṣer places this village between Haifa and Caesarea; it has not been located in the Arabic geographies. Le

Strange, 20, says it is Konaysa or Tell Kanisa, a few miles north of Athlit, which the Crusaders considered the site of Copernaum.

Kāzarun (Fārs): a town between Shirāz and the coast. See Yāqut, IV, 225; Abu'l-Fedā, 324.

Khabiṣ (Kermān): see Yāqut, II, 401; Abu'l-Fedā, 442.

Khān Lanjān (Isfahan): see Yāqut, II, 394; Abu'l-Fedā, 410.

Khandān: as described by Nāṣer, this place corresponds to the modern Kharzavil. See Dabir-Siyāqi, 236.

Kharzavil: the place mentioned by Nāser corresponds to the modern Kharzān, of which his "Khandān" may be a corruption. See Dabir-Siyāqi, 235.

Khayf (Arabia): see Yāqut, II, 508; Abu'l-Fedā, 81.

Khoy, Khway, Khowayy (Azerbaijan): see Yāqut, II, 502; Abu'l-Fedā, 396.

Kish, Kis, Qis: an island in the Indian Ocean. See Abu'l-Fedā, 372.

Laḥsā, al-Aḥsā' (Arabia, dependency of Bahrain): see Abu'l-Fedā, 98.

Lavāsān: name given to Damāvand according to Nāṣer.

Lurdajān, Lurdaghān (Ahwāz): see Yaqut, IV, 369.

Maʿarrat al-Noʿmān (Syria, Jond Ḥemṣ): see Yāqut, IV, 574; Abu'l-Fedā, 264.

Mahdiyya, al- (Maghreb, Efriqiyya): see Yāqut, IV, 693; Abu'l-Fedā, 144.

Mahrubān (Khuzestān on the Fārs border): see Yāqut, IV, 699; Abu'l-Fedā, 316.

Manbej (Syria, Jond Qennasrin): ancient Hieropolis. Same as the modern Syrian town of Membij. See Yāqut, IV, 654; Abu'l-Fedā, 270.

Marand (Azerbaijan): see Abu'l-Fedā, 400.

Marv Rud, Marw al-Rudh (Khorasan): see Yāqut, IV, 506; Abu'l-Fedā, 457.

Marv, Marw al-Shāhejān (Khorasan): see Yāqut, IV, 507; Abu'l-Feda, 446, 356.

Marwa: a mountain in Mecca. See Yāqut, IV, 513.

Mayyāfāreqin (Mesopotamia, Diyār Bakr): see Yāqut, IV, 703; Abu'l-Fedā, 278.

Mina, Menā (Arabia, Hejaz): a small town one farsang from Mecca. See Yāqut, IV, 642; Abu'l-Fedā, 81.

Moḥdatha (Mesopotamia, Diyār Bakr): a town north of Mayyāfāreqin, as described by Nāṣer. It is not mentioned in the geographies.

Mokrān (Sind): the coastal region bounded by Kermān and Sejestān. See Yāqut, IV, 612; Abu'l-Fedā, 348.

Mozdalefa, al- (Arabia, Hejaz): a place one farsang from Mina. See Yāqut, IV, 519.

Multan, Moltān (Hind): same as the modern town in Pakistan. See Yāqut, IV, 629; Abu'l-Fedā, 351.

Nā'in (Fārs): the modern Iranian town near Isfahan. See Yāqut, IV, 734.

Najrān (Arabia): see Yāqut, IV, 751; Abu'l-Fedā, 92.

Nishapur, Naysābur (Khorasan): see Yāqut, IV, 857; Abu'l-Fedā, 450.

Obolla (Iraq): see Yāqut, I, 96.

Panj Dēh: a collection of five villages near Marv Rud. See Yāqut, I, 743.

Piyāda, Biyādhaq: one of three villages, known as Seh Dēh, on the road between Isfahan and Nishapur; the other two are Jarmaq and Arāba. See Yāqut, II, 64.

Qā'en (Khorasan, Qohestān): see Yāqut, IV, 22; Abu'l-Fedā, 452.

Qapān: according to Yāqut, IV, 26, a village near Tabriz. The one described by Nāṣer is likely to be another of the same name between Qazvin and Ṭāram.

Qarul: no such name occurs in the geographies. From Nāṣer's description that it lies between Mayyāfāreqin and Manbej, this town should be Edessa (modern Urfa, in Turkey).

Qaryat al-ʿEnab (Palestine): Nāṣer describes this as a village between Laṭrun and Jerusalem. It has not been identified in the geographies.

Qatif (Arabia, dependency of Bahrein): see Yāqut, IV, 143; Abu'l-Fedā, 98.

Qayrawān (Maghreb, Efriqiyya): the modern Tunisian city and the area around it. See Yāqut, IV, 212; Abu'l-Fedā, 144.

Qazvin (Jabal): same as the modern Iranian city. See Yāqut, IV, 88; Abu'l-Fedā, 418.

Qef Onẓor: the name of a fort near Betlis.

Qennasrin, Qennesrin (Syria): see Yāqut, IV, 184; Abu'l-Fedā, 266.

Qobādiyān, Qobādhiyān (Balkh): see Yāqut, IV, 26; Abu'l-Fedā, 445.

Qods, al-: the Arabic name for Jerusalem.

Qolzom (Egypt): the ancient Clysma. See Yāqut, IV, 158; Abu'l-Fedā, 116.

Quha, Quhadh: the name of two large villages one stage from Rayy in the direction of Qazvin. See Yāqut, IV, 205.

Qumes, Kumash: the region extending from Besṭām to Semnān between Khorasan and Jebāl. See Yāqut, IV, 203; Abu'l-Fedā, 432.

Quṣ (Upper Egypt): see Yāqut, IV, 201; Abu'l-Fedā, 110.

Ramla (Palestine): see Yāqut, II, 817; Abu'l-Fedā, 240.
Raqqa (Qohestān): see Yāqut, II, 804.
Rostābād: according to Nāṣer, a village near Ṭabas. Dabir-Siyāqi suggests it may be the modern Dawlatābād east of Ṭabas.
Rumesh (?): the reading of this name is highly uncertain. The manuscripts seem to have "Rumesh" or "Hermes". According to Abu'l-Fedā, 39, the eastern branch of the Nile above the Tennis and Damietta lakes was known as Oshmun.

Ṣaʿda (Yemen): see Yāqut, III, 388.
Saʿidābād (Ṭabarestān): see Yāqut, III, 93.
Ṣāleḥiyya (Egypt): several towns by this name are given in Yāqut, III, 363, but none is in Egypt.
Samangān, Semenjān (Ṭokhārestān): a small town near Balkh. See Yāqut, III, 142; Abu'l-Fedā, 472.
Ṣanʿā (Yemen): same as the modern Yemeni city. See Yāqut, III, 420.
Sarāb, Sarāv (Azerbaijan): a city between Ardabil and Tabriz. See Yāqut, III, 64.
Sarakhs (Khorasan): a town between Nishapur and Marv. Same as the modern Iranian town. See Yāqut, III, 71; Abu'l-Fedā, 454.
Sarbā (Arabia): Nāṣer locates this place between Jazʿ and Falaj. It is not listed in the geographies.
Sarmin (Syria, dependency of Aleppo): see Yāqut, III, 83; Abu'l-Fedā, 264.
Saruj (Mesopotamia, Jazira): the modern Turkish town of Sürüç. See Yāqut, III, 85; Abu'l-Fedā, 276.
Sāva (Jabal): same as the modern Iranian town of Saveh. See Yāqut, III, 24; Abu'l-Fedā, 418.
Sejelmāsa (Maghreb): same as the modern town. See Yāqut, III, 45; Abu'l-Fedā, 136.
Semnān (Tabarestān, Qumes): town between Rayy and Dāmghān. See Yāqut, III, 141; Abu'l-Fedā, 436.
Shamirān (Tāram): see Yāqut, III, 148.
Shoburghān, Shobruqān (Balkh): see Yāqut, III, 254; Abu'l-Fedā, 446.
Sidon, Ṣaydā (Syria): same as the modern Lebanese town. See Yāqut, III, 439; Abu'l-Fedā, 248.

Ṭabas (Khorasan, Qohestān): same as the modern Iranian town. See Yāqut, III, 514; Abu'l-Fedā, 449.
Tabriz, Tebriz (Azerbaijan): same as the modern Iranian city. See Yāqut, II, 822; Abu'l-Fedā, 400.
Ṭā'ef (Arabia, Hejaz): same as the modern town. See Yāqut, III, 494; Abu'l-Fedā, 94.

Ṭālaqān (Khorasan): see Yāqut, III, 491; Abu'l-Fedā, 458.

Ṭarāborzon (Syria): Nāṣer names this town as being between Tripoli and Byblos, the site of the modern Batrun. The name appears to be a corruption of the Greek name for the site, Θεου Πρόσωπον. See Dussaud, 71.

Ṭāram, Ṭārom: the region between Qazvin and Gilān. See Yāqut, I, 811.

Tavva, Tawwaj, Tawwaz (Fārs): a town near Kāzarun. See Yāqut, I, 890; Abu'l-Fedā, 326.

Tehāma (southern Hejaz): see Yāqut, I, 901; Abu'l-Fedā, 78.

Tennis: an island off the coast of Egypt in the Mediterranean. See Yāqut, I, 882; Abu'l-Fedā, 118.

Tiberias, Ṭabariyya (Syria, Jordan): see Yāqut, II, 509; Abu'l-Fedā, 242.

Ṭina, al- (Egypt): see Yāqut, III, 572; Abu'l:Fedā, 103.

Thorayyā (Arabia): Nāṣer places it between Ṭā'ef and Falaj. Not identified in other sources.

Tripoli, Ṭarābolos al-Shām (Syria): same as the modern Lebanese city. See Yāqut, III, 521; Abu'l-Fedā, 252.

Tun (Khorasan, Quhestān): same as the modern Iranian town. See Abu'l-Fedā, 444.

Tyre, Ṣur (Syria): the ancient city and modern Lebanese town. See Yāqut, III, 433; Abu'l-Fedā, 242.

Vān (Armenia): see Yāqut, IV, 895; Abu'l-Fedā, 389.

Vasṭān, Wosṭān (Armenia): see Abu'l-Fedā, 396.

Wādi al-Qorā (Arabia): see Yāqut, IV, 878; Abu'l-Fedā, 89, 80.

Yamāma (Arabia, Hejaz): see Abu'l-Fedā, 96.

Zabid (Yemen): see Yāqut, II, 915; Abu'l-Fedā, 88.

Zuzan (Khorasan, Qohestān): see Yāqut, II, 958; Abu'l-Fedā, 452.

Glossary of Terms

Bāz: Nāṣer explains that towns on the Red Sea are called *bāz*. The *Borhān-e qāṭeʿ*, I, 218, gives as one meaning of *bāz* "the course of a flood," which would be *wādi* in Arabic. The word may have some connection with the Persian *bāj* or *bāzh(gāh)*, a toll or customs station.

Kharvār: a donkey-load. See Appendix B.

Kashkāb: reconstituted dried milk curd, used for refreshment and medicinal purposes.

Khān: a caravanserai.

Maqṣura: an enclosed portion of a mosque generally reserved for the ruler. The enclosures are normally surrounded by latticed screens and were originally designed to protect the ruler from assassination while in attendance at the mosque.

Mashhad: A shrine to commemorate the martyrdom of Ḥosayn b. ʿAli b. Abi Ṭāleb, grandson of the Prophet; also used loosely for any shrine devoted to a martyr.

Meḥrāb: a niche in a mosque to indicate the *qebla*, q.v.; also, especially in the Dome of the Rock area in Jerusalem, used for oratory.

Mojāwer: a person who resides, temporarily or permanently, near a holy place or shrine in order to receive the blessing attendant upon the sacred spot.

Nawrōz (modern Persian *nowruz*): the Persian New Year's Day, which occurs on the vernal equinox, from which the new year is reckoned.

Qebla: the direction of the Kaʿba in Mecca, toward which Muslims orient themselves when they pray. Nāṣer often gives directions in terms of the *qebla*, which could be any direction, depending upon where he is.

Rakʿat: a "cycle" of liturgical prayer consisting of recitation, bowing, kneeling and prostration. The canonical daily prayers have varying numbers of *rakʿat*s prescribed for them.

Rebāṭ: a type of frontier post *cum* caravanserai.

Saʿy: a portion of the Pilgrimage ritual wherein the pilgrim runs between Mount Ṣafā' and Mount Marwa seven times in order to commemorate Hagar's frantic search for water in the desert for her son Ishmael.

Sharif: "noble," loosely used to designate any descendant of the Prophet Moḥammad.

Zayt ḥārr: oil derived from vegetable seed and used for lamps.

APPENDIX A. Calendrical Systems

THE CALENDRICAL SYSTEMS USED BY NĀṢER-E KHOSRAW

The calendar adopted by Islam and by which daily life and all religious occasions were reckoned is the Arabian lunar calendar, which consists of twelve lunar months of 29½ days each. Since the months are based on the cycles of the moon, no easily calculable correspondence exists between the lunar and the solar calendar, and the lunar year recedes approximately eleven days every solar year. The names of the Islamic lunar months, beginning with the first, are as follows:

1. Moḥarram	5. Jomādā I	9. Ramaḍān
2. Ṣafar	6. Jomādā II	10. Shawwāl
3. Rabiʿ I	7. Rajab	11. Dhu'l-Qaʿda
4. Rabiʿ II	8. Shaʿbān	12. Dhu'l-Ḥejja

Since a lunar calendar is impractical for fiscal purposes, the Old Persian solar calendar was retained by the bureaucracy in the eastern Islamic realms, as was the Syrian calendar in the eastern Mediterranean lands. By the time of Nāṣer-e Khosraw, the Old Persian months, which originally corresponded to the signs of the Zodiac, had "slipped" forward by precession of the equinoxes almost twenty days. As later reformed by ʿOmar Khayyām, the modern Persian months are:

Farvardin = Aries (21 March–20 April)
Ordibehesht = Taurus (20 April–21 May)
Khordād = Gemini (22 May–21 June)
Tir = Cancer (22 June–22 July)
Mordād = Leo (23 July–22 August)
Shahrivar = Virgo (23 August–22 September)
Mehr = Libra (23 September–22 October)
Abān = Scorpio (23 October–21 November)
Adhar = Sagittarius (22 November–21 December)
Day = Capricorn (22 December–20 January)
Bahman = Aquarius (21 January–19 February)
Esfand = Pisces (20 February–20 March)

Since Nāṣer quotes from the unreformed Old Calendar, his dates are approximately twenty days ahead of the reformed calendar.

In Islamic reckoning the day begins at sunset; therefore, what we would call "Monday night" would be "Tuesday eve" to Nāṣer. Even taking into consideration the confusion that arises from this fact, it has not been possible to reconcile all the days of the week as given in the *Safarnāma*. Although the best conversion tables have been consulted and variant readings in the extant manuscripts have been reviewed, quite often his "Saturday the 5th" converts into a Wednesday when calculated in the Christian calendar. The days of the week have therefore been left as they stand in the Persian text; only the Islamic date has been converted into its Christian equivalent and added between square brackets.

APPENDIX B. Weights and Measures

UNITS OF LINEAR MEASURE

The "cubit" (*arash*, also *arsh*) is defined as the distance from the tip of the middle finger to the elbow, which would be about 1½ feet, In practice, on the basis of measurements still available from the Dome of the Rock in Jerusalem, the "cubit" would appear to be roughly equal to 2 feet. The "legal cubit" (*dherāʿ shar'i*) is usually defined as 49.875 cm. (19.6″).

The "ell" (*gaz*) is defined as 24 fingers, or 1½ feet, but it seems to be used interchangeably by Nāṣer as equivalent to the "cubit" and should therefore be reckoned from 1½ to 2 feet.

The "parasang" (*farsang, farsakh*) is the distance traveled by a caravan in one hour; it is 3 miles of 4000 *gaz* each, or 12,000 *gaz*, equal to a little less than 3½ modern miles (6 km).

UNITS OF WEIGHT

Units of weight have been so varied in different locales and at different periods of time in the Islamic world that it is only with trepidation that the following approximations are offered. See Walther Hinz, *Islamische Masse und Gewichte* (Leiden, 1955).

1 dang (dāneq, dānak) = 8 grains
4 dāngs = 1 dirhem
6 dāngs = 1 mithqāl (approximately 1 3/7 dram)
15 mithqals = 1 seer
40 seers = 1 maund (roughly 3½ lbs.)
100 maunds = 1 kharvār (roughly 350 lbs.)

CURRENCY

Nāṣer quotes prices in dinars, which, unless explicitly stated as the Nishapur gold dinar, means the Fatimid "Maghrebi dinar" struck in Egypt. He gives the relative value of the two as 1 Maghrebi dinar equal to 1 1/6 Nishapuri dinar.

APPENDIX C. *Nāṣer's Itinerary*

First Administrative Trip

Marv
Panj Deh, Marv Rud
Juzjānān
Shoburghān
Fāryāb district
Samangān
Ṭālaqān
Marv Rud
Marv

Travels

Sarakhs
Nishapur

QUMES
Gavān
Besṭām
Dāmghān
Ābkhwari
Chāshtkhwārān
Semnān
Damāvand
Quha
Qazvin
Bil
Qapān

DAYLAM
Kharzavil

ṬĀRAM
Baraz al-Khayr
Khandān
Shamirān

AZERBAIJAN
Sarāb
Saʿidābād
Tabriz
Khoy

ARMENIA
Bargri
Vān
Vasṭān
Akhlāṭ
Betlis
Arzan

DIYĀR BAKR
Mayyāfāreqin
Āmed
Ḥarrān
Qarul (Edessa ?)

SYRIA
Saruj
Manbej
Aleppo
Jond Qennasrin
Sarmin
Maʿarrat al-Noʿmān
Kafr Ṭāb
Ḥamā
ʿErqa
Tripoli
Ṭarāborzon
Byblos
Beirut
Sidon
Tyre

PALESTINE
Acre
al-Berwa
Dammun (?)
Eʿbellin
Ḥaẓira
Irbid
Tiberias
Kafr Kanna
Acre
Haifa
Kanisa (?)
Caesarea
Kafr Sābā
Kafr Sallām
Ramla
Latrun
Qaryat al-ʿEnab
Jerusalem
Bethlehem
Hebron
Jerusalem

	ʿArʿar		Falaj
	Wādi al-Qorā		Yamāma
[*First Hajj*]	Mecca		Laḥsā
	Jerusalem	IRAQ	Basra
	Ramla		Shāṭe' ʿOthmān
	Ascalon		ʿAbbādān
EGYPT	Ṭina	FĀRS	Mahrubān
	Tennis		Arrajān
	Ṣāleḥiyya		Shamshir-borid
	Cairo		Lurdagān
	Al-Jār		Khān Lanjān
	Medina	JEBĀL	Isfahan
[*Second Hajj*]	Mecca		Haythamābād
	Cairo		
	Qolzom	BIĀBĀN	Nā'in
[*Third Hajj*]	Mecca		Garma
	Cairo	QOHESTĀN	Ṭabas
	Asyuṭ		Raqqa
	Akhmim		Tun
	Quṣ		Qā'en
	Aswān	KHORASAN	Sarakhs
	Ḍayqa		Marv Rud
	Ḥawḍ (?)		Ābgarm
	ʿAydhāb		Bāryāb
ARABIA	Jidda		Samangān
[*Fourth Hajj*]	Mecca		Seh Darra
	Ṭā'ef		Dastgerd
	Thorayyā		Miyān Rustā
	Jazʿ		Balkh

Bibliography of Works Cited

Abu'l-Fedā ʿEmād al-Din Esmāʿil. *Taqwim al-boldān*. Edited by Reinaud and Baron MacGuckin de Slane. Paris, L'Imprimerie Royale, 1840.

Azraqi, Abu'l-Walid Moḥammad b. ʿAbd Allāh al-. *Akhbār Makka*. Edited by Roshdi al-Ṣāleḥ Malḥas. Mecca, Dār al-Thaqāfa, 1385/1965.

Berchem, Max van. *Amida: Matériaux pour l'épigraphie et l'histoire musulmanes du Diyar-bekr*. Heidelberg, C. Winter, 1910.

———. *Matériaux pour un corpus inscriptionum arabicarum*. Jerusalem, 1923.

———. *Voyage en Syrie*. Cairo, L'Institut Français d'Archéologie Orientale, 1914–15.

Burton, Sir Richard F. *Personal Narrative of a Pilgrimage to al-Madinah & Meccah*. 2 volumes. New York, Dover, 1964.

Creswell, K. A. C. *The Muslim Architecture of Egypt*. Volume 1. New York, Hacket Art Books, 1978.

Dussaud, R. *Topographie historique de la Syrie antique et médiévale*. Bibliothèque Archaeologique et Historique, 4. Paris, Geuthner, 1927.

Ebn Jobayr, Abu'l-Ḥosayn Moḥammad. *Reḥlat Ebn Jobayr*. Beirut, Dār Ṣāder, 1384/1964.

Hodgson, Marshall G. S. *The Order of Assassins; The Struggle of the Early Nizârî Ismâʿîlîs against the Islamic World*. The Hague, Mouton, 1955.

Hütteroth, Wolf-Dieter, and Kamal Abdulfattah. *Historical Geography of Palestine, Transjordan and Southern Syria in the Late 16th Century*. Erlanger Geographische Arbeiten, Sonderband 5. Erlangen, 1977.

Karagi, Mohammad al-. *La Civilisation des eaux cachées*. Edited and translated by Aly Mazaheri. Nice, L'Institut d'Etudes et de Recherches Interethniques et Interculturelles, 1973.

Kesā'i, al-. *Tales of the Prophets of al-Kisa'i*. Translated by W. M. Thackston. Boston, Twayne, 1978.

Lewis, Bernard. *The Origins of Ismāʿīlism*. Cambridge, Cambridge University Press, 1944.

Maqrizi, Taqi al-Din Aḥmad b. ʿAli al-. *Ketāb al-kheṭaṭ al-maqriziyya*. al-Shiyāḥ, Eḥyā' al-ʿOlum, n.d.

Moḥammad b. Ḥosayn b. Khalaf Tabrizi. *Borhān-e qāṭeʿ*. 5 volumes. Edited by Moḥammad Moʿin. Tehran, Ebn-e Sinā, 1330–42/1951–63.

Nahrwāli, Qoṭb al-Din Moḥammad. *al-Eʿlām be-aʿlām bayt allāh al-ḥarām*. Mecca, ʿElmiyya, 1370/1950.

Ravaisse, Paul. "Essai sur l'histoire et sur la topographie du Caire d'après Maḳrīzī." *Mémoires publiés par les membres de la Mission archéologique française au Caire*. Paris, Leroux. Vol. 1 (1886): 409–479; vol. 3 (1889): 1–114.

Yāqut b. ʿAbd Allāh al-Ḥamawi, Abu ʿAbd Allāh. *Moʿjam al-boldān*. Edited by Ferdinand Wüstenfeld. 6 volumes. Leipzig, Brockhaus, 1886–70.

A Bibliography of Nāṣer-e Khosraw

A. Works by Nāṣer-e Khosraw:

Divān. Editions: (1) Tabriz, 1280/1864. (2) Edited by Zayn al-ʿĀbedin al-Sharif al-Ṣafavi. Tehran, 1314/1896. (3) Cawnpore, Nawal Kishore, 1912. (4) Edited by Mojtabā Minovi. Tehran, 1304–07/1925–28. (5) Edited by Sayyed Naṣr Allāh Taqavi and Sayyed Ḥasan Taqizāda. Tehran, 1307/1929. (6) Edited by Mahdi Sohayli. Isfahan, Ta'yid, 1339/1960. Selections and Translations: (1) "Auswahl aus Nâṣir Chusrau's Ḳaṣiden." Translated by Hermann Ethé. In *Zeitschrift der deutschen morgenländischen Gesellschaft* 36 (1882): 478–508. (2) "Kürzere Lieder und poetische Fragmente aus Nâçir Khusraus Dîvân." Translated by Hermann Ethé. In *Nachrichten der Gesellschaft der Wissenschaften* (Göttingen, 1882): 124–52. (3) *Pānzdah qaṣida az Ḥakim Naṣer-e Khosraw-e Qobādiyāni*. Edited by Mahdi Moḥaqqeq. Tehran, Ṭahuri, 1340/1961. (4) *Forty Poems from the Divan*. Translated by Peter Lamborn Wilson and Gholam-Reza Aavani. Tehran, Imperial Iranian Academy of Philosophy, 1977.

Goshāyesh-o rahāyesh. (1) Edited by Saʿid Nafisi. Ismaili Society Series A, no. 5. Bombay and Leiden, 1950. (3) *Il Libro dello scioglimento e della liberazione*. Translated by Pio Filippani-Ronconi. Naples, Istituto Universitario Orientali, 1959.

Jāmeʿ al-ḥekmatayn. Edited by Henry Corbin and Moḥammad Moʿin. Tehran, Institut Franco-Iranien, 1953.

Khʷān al-ekhwān. (1) Edited by Yaḥya al-Khashshāb. Cairo, L'Institut Français d'Archéologie Orientale, 1940. (2) Edited by ʿ. Qavim. Tehran, Bārāni, 1338/1959.

Rawshanā'ināma. Editions: (1) Edited by Hermann Ethē. "Nâṣir Chusrau's Rûshanâinâma, oder Buch der Erleuchtung in Text und Uebersetzung, nebst Noten und kritisch-biographischem Appendix." In *ZDMG* 33 (1879): 645–65, 34 (1880): 617–42. (2) Berlin, 1341/1923. (3) Tehran, 1304–07/1925–28. (4) *Resāla-ye shesh faṣl, yā Rawshanā'ināma*. Edited by W. Ivanow. Cairo, Maṭbaʿat al-Kāteb al-Meṣri, 1948. (5) *Six Chapters or Shish Fasl, Also Called Rawshana'inama*. Edited and translated by W. Ivanow. Leiden, Brill, 1949.

Saʿādatnāma. (1) "Le Livre de la Félicité." Edited and translated by E. Fagnan. In *ZDMG* 34 (1880): 643–74. (2) Berlin, 1341/1923. (3) Tehran, 1304–07/1925–28.

Safarnāma. Editions: (1) *Sefer nameh; relation du voyage de Nassiri Khosrau*. Edited by Charles Schefer. Paris, Ernest Leroux, 1881. (2) Delhi, 1882. (3) Bombay, 1309/1892. (3) Tehran, 1312/1894–95 by Zayn al-ʿĀbedin al-Sharif al-Ṣafavi. (4) Edited by M. Ghanizada. Berlin, Kaviani, 1341/1922. (5) Edited by Moḥammad Dabir-Siyāqi. First edition, second printing. Tehran, Zovvār, 1335/1957. (6) Edited by Moḥammad Dabir-Siyāqi. Second edition. Selsele-ye Enteshārāt-e Anjoman-e Athār-e Melli, 120. Tehran, Chāpkhāne-ye Dāneshgāh-e Tehrān, 1354/1976. (7) Edited by Nāder Vazinpur. Tehran, Ketābhā-ye Jibi, 1971. Translations: (1) "An Account of Jerusalem Translated . . . from the Persian text of Násir ibn Khusru's Safar-námah." Translated by A. R. Fuller. In *Journal of the Royal Asiatic Society* (1873): 142ff. (2) *Sefer nameh; relation du voyage de Nassiri Khosrau.* Translated by Charles Schefer. Paris, Ernest Leroux, 1881. (3) *Diary of a Journey through Syria and Palestine by Nâsir-i-Khusrau, in 1047 A.D.* Translated by Guy Le Strange. London, Library of the Palestine Pilgrims' Text Society, 1893. (4) *Safarnāma.* Translated by Yaḥyā al-Khashshāb. Cairo, Lajnat al-Ta'lif, 1365/1945. (5) Transcribed into Tajik. *Safarnoma; kniga puteshestviia.* Dushanbe, Irfon, 1970.

Wajh-e din. (1) Berlin, Kaviani, 1343/1925. (2) Tehran, Ṭahuri, 1348/1969. (3) Edited by Gholām-Rezā Aʿvāni. Tehran, Imperial Iranian Academy of Philosophy, 2536/1977.

Zād al-mosāferin. Edited by M. Badhl al-Raḥmān. Berlin, Kaviani, 1341/1923.

B. Studies, Secondary Works, etc.

Ashurov, Gafar Ashurovich. *Filosofskie vzglyady Nosiri Xusrava; na osnove analiza traktata "Zad-al-musafirin."* Dushanbe, 1965.

Bertel's, Andrei Evgen'evich. *Nasir-i Khosrov i ismailizm.* Moscow, Izd-vo Vostochnoi Lit-ry, 1959.

Corbin, Henry. *Etude préliminarie pur Le livre réunissant les deux sagesses.* Tehran, Institut Franco-Iranien, 1953.

———. "Le 'Kitāb Jāmiʿ al-Ḥikmatayn' de Nāṣir-e Khosraw." *Proceedings of the 22nd Congress of Orientalists.* Leiden, 1957. Vol. 2, pp. 241–242.

Ḥāli, Khʷāja Moḥammad Alṭāf-Ḥosayn. *Moqaddama-ye Safarnāma-ye Ḥakim Nāṣer-e Khosraw.* In Persian with Urdu translation by Moḥammad Ṣeddiq Ṭāher Shādāni. Lahore, Majles-e Taraqqi-ye Adab, 1973.

Ivanow, Vladimir Alekseevich. *Nasir-i Khusraw and Ismailism.* Leiden, Brill, 1948.

———. *Problems in Nasir-i Khusraw's Biography.* Ismaili Society Series B, no. 10. Bombay, 1956.

al-Khashab, Yahya. *Nasir è Hosraw; son voyage, sa pensée religieuse, sa philosophie et sa poésie.* Cairo, P. Barbey, 1940.

Kongre-ye Jahāni-ye Nāṣer-e Khosraw. *Yādnāme-ye Nāṣer-e Khosraw.* Mashhad, Dāneshgāh-e Ferdawsi, 2535/1976.

Mohaghegh, Mehdi. "Nāṣir-i Khusraw and His Spiritual *Nisbah.*" *Yādnāme-ye Irāni-ye Minorsky* (1969): pp. 143–148.

Moḥaqqeq, Mahdi. *Taḥlil-e ash'ār-e Nāṣer-e Khosraw.* Tehran, Tehran University Press, 1344/1965.

Ṭarzi, 'Abd al-Wahhāb. *Nāṣer-e Khosraw-e Balkhi: ḥakim-o shā'er-e qarn-e panjom-e hejri-ye Afghānestān.* Kabul, Bayhaqi, 1355 [1976].

Persian Heritage Series

Attar, *Muslim Saints & Mystics* (No. 1), tr. A. J. Arberry
University of Chicago Press, 1966 (Reprint 1973)

Nezami, *Chosroès et Chirine* (No. 2), tr. Henri Massé
Maisonneuve et Larose, Paris, 1970

Rumi, *Mystical Poems I* (No. 3), tr. A. J. Arberry
University of Chicago Press, 1974

Varavini, *The Tales of Marzuban* (No. 4), tr. Reuben Levy
Indiana Univ. Press, 1959 (Reprint 1968)

Tusi, *The Nasirean Ethics* (No. 5), tr. G. M. Wickens
George Allen & Unwin, London, 1964

Nezami, *Le Sette Principesse* (No. 6), tr. A. Bausani
Leonardo da Vinci, Rome, 1967

Ferdowsi, *The Epic of the Kings* (No. 7), tr. Reuben Levy
University of Chicago Press, 1967 (Reprint 1973)

Aruzi, *Les quatre discours* (No. 8), tr. I. de Gastines
Maisonneuve et Larose, Paris, 1968

Anon., *The Letter of Tansar* (No. 9), tr. M. Boyce
IsMEO, Rose, 1968

Rashid al-Din, *The Successors of Genghis Khan* (No. 10)
tr. J. A. Boyle, Columbia University Press, 1971

Mohammad ibn Ibrahim, *The Ship of Sulaiman* (No. 11)
tr. J. O'Kane, Columbia University Press, 1972

Faramarz, *Samak-e Ayyar* (No. 12), tr. F. Razavi
Maisonneuve et Larose, Paris, 1972

Avicenna, *Metaphysica* (No. 13), tr. P. Morewedge
Columbia University Press, 1973

Gurgani, *Vis and Ramin* (No. 14), tr. G. Morrison
Columbia University Press, 1972

Fasai, *History of Persia Under Qajar Rule* (No. 15)
tr. H. Busse, Columbia University Press, 1972

Aturpat-e Emetan, *Dēnkart III* (No. 16), tr. J. De Menasce
Libraire Klincksieck, Paris, 1974

Sa'di, *Bustan* (No. 17), tr. G. M. Wickens
University of Toronto Press, 1974

Anon., *Folk Tales of Ancient Persia* (No. 18)
tr. F. Hekmat & Y. Lovelock, Caravan Books, Delmar, N.Y., 1974

Bighami, *Love and War* (No. 19), tr. W. Hanaway, Jr.
Scholars' Facsimiles & Reprints, Delmar, N.Y., 1974

Anon., *The History of Sistan* (No. 20), tr. M. Gold
IsMEO, Rome, 1977

Manichaean Literature (An Anthology) (No. 22), tr. J. Asmussen
Scholars' Facsimiles & Reprints, Delmar, N.Y., 1974

Mystical Poems of Rūmī, 2nd Selection (No. 23), tr. A. J. Arberry
Westview Press, Boulder, Colorado, 1979

Rumi, *Le Livre du Dedans* (No. 25), tr. E. de Vitray-Meyerovitch
Edition Sinbad, Paris, 1975

Rumi, *Licht und Reigen* (No. 26), tr. J. Ch. Bûrgel
Herbert Lang Verlag, Bern, 1974

Samarkandi, *Le Livre des sept vizirs* (No. 27), tr. D. Bogdanovic
Edition Sinbad, Paris, 1975

Monshi, *History of Shah 'Abbas* (No. 28), tr. R. M. Savory
Westview Press, Boulder, Colorado 1979

Attar, *Ilahiname* (No. 29), tr. J. A. Boyle
Manchester University Press, 1977

Hafez, *Divan (Hafizu-Shishu)* (No. 30), tr. T. Kuriyanagi
Heibosha Ltd., Tokyo, 1977

Anon., *Iskandarnamah* (No. 31), tr. M. Southgate
Columbia University Press, 1978

Nezam al-Molk, *The Book of Government* (No. 32), revised
tr. H. Darke, Routledge and Kegan Paul, London, 1978

Nezami, *Khosrau and Shirin* (in Japanese) (No. 33), tr. A. Okada
Heibosha Ltd., Tokyo, 1977

Aturpāt-i Emētān, *The Wisdom of the Sasanian Sagas (Dēnkard VI)*
(No. 34), tr. S. Shaked, Westview Press, Boulder, Colorado, 1979

Razi, *The Path of God's Bondsmen (Merṣād al-'Ebād)* (No. 35)
tr. H. Algar, Westview Press, Boulder, Colorado, 1980

Tabari, *History (774–809 A.D.)*,translated and annotated by a number
of scholars, SUNY Press, 1985 vols. 2, 18, 27, 35, 38

In Press

Mohammad b. Monavvar, *The Tales of Abū Sa'īd (Asrār al-Towhīd)* (No. 36), tr. J. O'Kane, Westview Press, Boulder, Colorado

Ferdausi, *Anthologie du livre des rois* (No. 37) tr. J. Mohl. ed. G. Lazard

Forthcoming

Nishaburi, *History of the Saljuqs (Saljūqnāma)* (No. 24) tr. K. A. Luther

Anon., *Sasanian Law Book (Mātikān-ī hazār dātastān)* tr. A. Perikhanian and N. Garsoian

Anon., *Myths and Legends of Ancient Iran,* tr. E. Yarshater

Persian Studies Series

Reuben Levy, *Introduction to Persian Literature* (unnumbered) Columbia University Press, 1969

Ali Dashti, *In Search of Omar Khayyam* (No. 1), tr. L. P. Elwell-Sutton George Allen and Unwin, London, 1971

James Pearson, *A Bibliography of Pre-Islamic Persia* (No. 2) Mansell Information and Publishing, London, 1975

Christopher J. Brunner, *A Syntax of Western Middle Iranian* (No. 3) Caravan Books, Delmar, New York, 1977

John Yohannan, *Persian Literature in England and America* (No. 4) Caravan Books, Delmar, New York 1977

J. Ch. Bürgel, *Drei Hafis Studien* (No. 5) Herbert Lang Verlag, Bern, 1975

M. H. Tabataba'i, *Shi'ite Islam* (No. 6), tr. S. H. Nasr State University of New York Press, Albany, 1975

Clifford Edmund Bosworth, *The Later Ghaznavids* (No. 7) Edinburgh University Press and Colujmbia University Press, 1978

A. Schimmel, *The Triumphal Sun. A Study of the Works of Jalāladdin Rumi* (No. 8), Fine Books, London, 1978

M. J. McDermott, *The Theology of al-Shaikh al-Mufid* (No. 9) Dar el-Machreq, Beirut, 1978

Biruni: A Symposium, ed. E. Yarshater and D. Bishop (No. 10) Columbia University, 1976

Modern Persian Literature Series

Karimi-Hakkak, *An Anthology of Modern Persian Poetry* (No. 1) 1978

Sadeq Hedayat: An Anthology (No. 2) tr. B. Spooner, H. Darke, G. Kapucinski, et al. Westview Press, Boulder, Colorado, 1979

Al-e Ahmad, *Plaqued by the West* (No. 4) tr. Paul Sprachman

Farrokhzad, *Bride of Acacias* (No. 5) tr. J. Kessler and A. Banani

Jamalzadeh, *Once Upon a Time* (No. 6) tr. Professor H. Moayyad and Paul Sprachman

Sholevar, *The Night's Journey* and *The Coming of the Messiah* (No. 7) tr. by the author Concourse Press, Philadelphia (1984)

Forthcoming

An Anthology of Modern Persian Drama, tr. G. Kapucinski

Alavi, *Her Eyes,* tr. J. O'Kane

Persian Art Series

Published

Highlights of Persian Art, ed. R. Ettinghausen and E. Yarshater Westview Press, Boulder, Colorado, 1979 (No. 1)

Forthcoming

Sasanian Art, V. Lukonin, P. Harper, D. Huff, G. Azarpay.

Index